ANCIENT HISTORY ATLAS

OTHER ATLASES IN THIS SERIES, BY MARTIN GILBERT

Recent History Atlas 1860–1960
British History Atlas
American History Atlas
Jewish History Atlas
First World War Atlas

Forthcoming

Russian History Atlas

ANCIENT HISTORY ATLAS

Michael Grant

Cartography by ARTHUR BANKS

Weidenfeld and Nicolson
5 Winsley Street London W1

ISBN 0 297 99372 0   Paperback
ISBN 0 297 99371 1   Cased
Printed in Great Britain by
C. Tinling & Co. Ltd, London and Prescot.

Preface

This is, in the first place, an atlas of the classical world – the ancient Greek and Roman world, which needs to be understood if we are to understand the world of today. To say that such an atlas could ever be a substitute for a historical survey would be an exaggeration. Nevertheless, geography is such a vital, indeed predominant, factor in ancient history – and such a difficult factor because of all the changes of names[1] – that the whole course of events often seems to mean practically nothing without maps, and without a lot of them, carefully devised.

Older classical atlases, apart from a varying degree of emphasis on physical aspects, tended to concentrate on political themes, and it is true enough that these stand in great need of maps. But the present volume attempts to cast the net wider, and to introduce economic, cultural, religious and other topics as well. There are also a number of town plans.

Modern research in archaeology and other fields has shown that the classical world cannot be grasped without some appreciation of what went before it. I have consequently started this book with a number of maps illustrating the Mediterranean world during the second millennium BC, and particularly during the period from 1700 BC onwards, when the international scene had already assumed a well-defined and complex appearance; and the story is carried onwards to offer brief illustrations of the Old Testament. At the other end of the story, the traditional terminal date of the ancient world, the year AD 476 when the last western emperor ceased to reign, is again not a very meaningful landmark, so I have carried on the tale until the reign of Justinian in the following century.

It will be clear enough what a very great deal is owed to the talent of Mr Arthur Banks for transcribing the written and spoken word into cartographic form. I am also most grateful to Mr Julian Shuckburgh for all the assistance he has rendered on behalf of the publishers, and I want to thank Miss Jane Dorner for assistance with the index. Finally, I have to acknowledge a substantial debt to existing classical atlases, German and English. And I must single out, for a special word of gratitude, the *Atlas of the Classical World* edited by A. A. M. van der Heyden and H. H. Scullard for Messrs Nelson, and *Westermanns Grosser Atlas zur Weltgeschichte* (Westermann, Braunschweig). They have both given me ideas and material for a number of maps.

MICHAEL GRANT
Gattaiola

1971

[1] Modern names are given after the ancient in the Index.

List of Maps

1

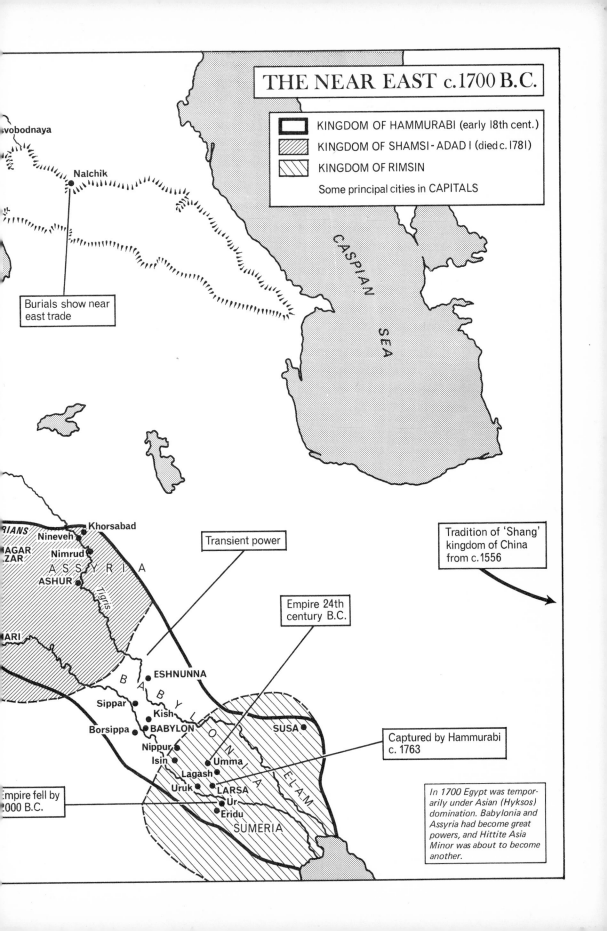

THE NEAR EAST c.1700 B.C.

▭ KINGDOM OF HAMMURABI (early 18th cent.)

▨ KINGDOM OF SHAMSI - ADAD I (died c.1781)

▨ KINGDOM OF RIMSIN

Some principal cities in CAPITALS

svobodnaya

Nalchik

CASPIAN SEA

Burials show near east trade

Tradition of 'Shang' kingdom of China from c.1556

Khorsabad

Nineveh

RIANS

AGAR
ZAR

Nimrud

ASSYRIA

ASHUR

Tigris

Transient power

Empire 24th century B.C.

MARI

BABYLON

ESHNUNNA

Sippar

Kish

Borsippa

BABYLON

SUSA

Captured by Hammurabi c. 1763

Nippur

Isin

Umma

Lagash

ELAM

Uruk

LARSA

Empire fell by
2000 B.C.

Ur

Eridu

SUMERIA

In 1700 Egypt was temporarily under Asian (Hyksos) domination. Babylonia and Assyria had become great powers, and Hittite Asia Minor was about to become another.

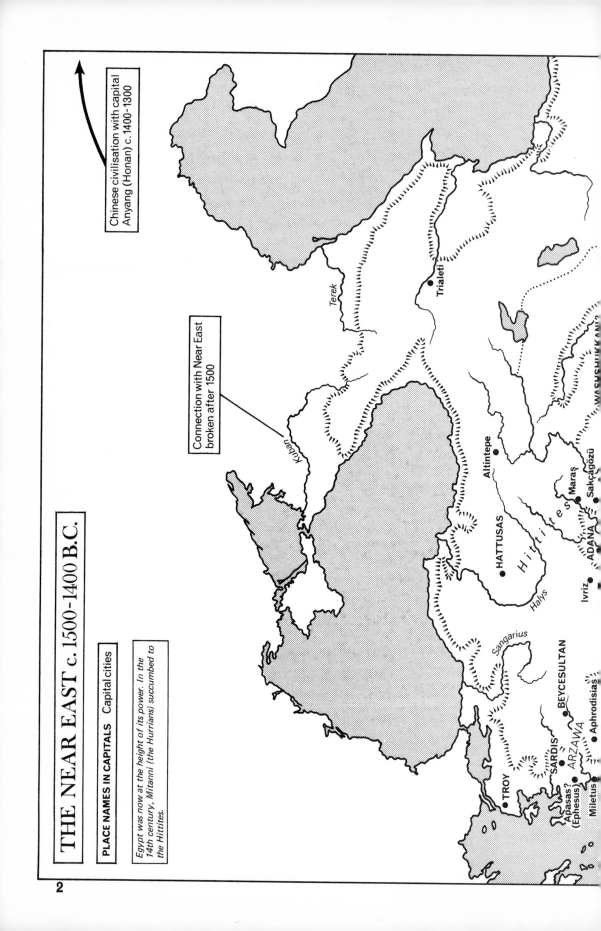

THE NEAR EAST c. 1500–1400 B.C.

PLACE NAMES IN CAPITALS   Capital cities

Egypt was now at the height of its power. In the 14th century, Mitanni (the Hurrians) succumbed to the Hittites.

Chinese civilisation with capital Anyang (Honan) c. 1400–1300

Connection with Near East broken after 1500

Trialeti

Terek

Kuban

Altintepe

HATTUSAS

H i t t i t e s

Maraş

Sakçagözü

ADANA

WASHSHUKANI?

Ivriz

Halys

Sangarius

BEYCESULTAN

SARDIS

ARZAWA

Aphrodisias

TROY

Apasas? (Ephesus)

Miletus

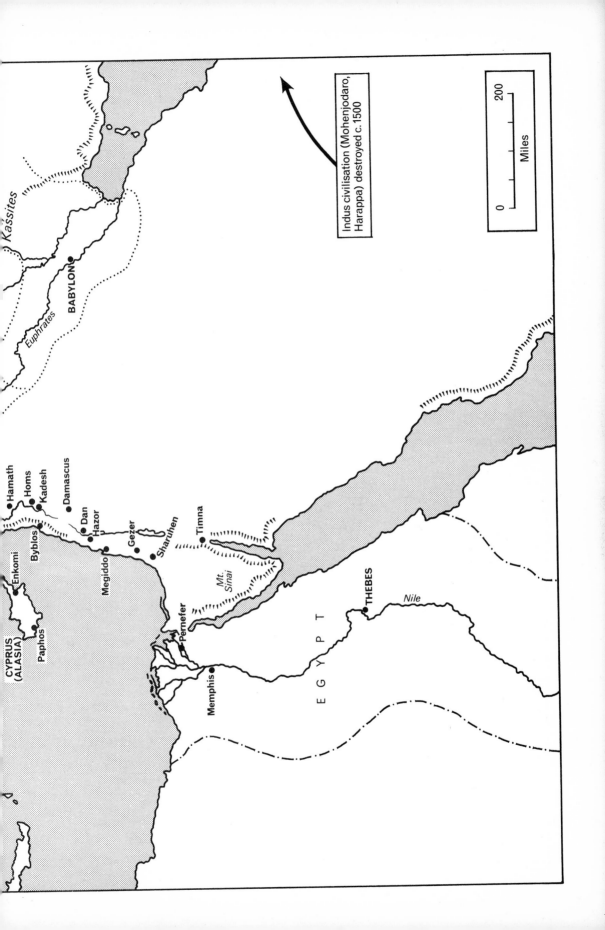

Indus civilisation (Mohenjodaro, Harappa) destroyed c. 1500

200

Miles

0

Kassites

BABYLON

Euphrates

Hamath

Homs

Kadesh

Damascus

Dan

Hazor

Byblos

Gezer

Sharuhen

Timna

Enkomi

Megiddo

Mt. Sinai

CYPRUS
(ALASIA)

Paphos

Pernefer

THEBES

Nile

E G Y P T

Memphis

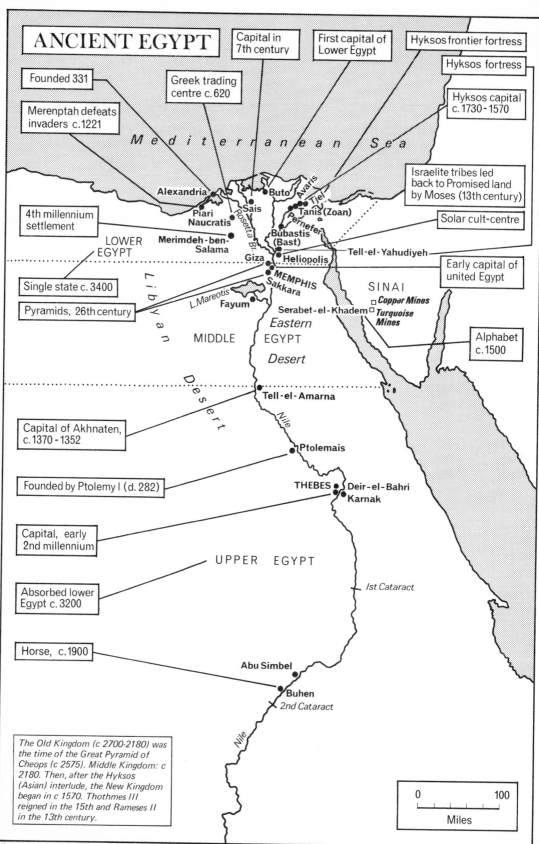

ANCIENT EGYPT

Capital in 7th century

First capital of Lower Egypt

Hyksos frontier fortress

Hyksos fortress

Founded 331

Greek trading centre c. 620

Hyksos capital c. 1730 - 1570

Merenptah defeats invaders c.1221

Mediterranean Sea

Israelite tribes led back to Promised land by Moses (13th century)

Alexandria

Buto

Avaris

Tjel

4th millennium settlement

Piari
Naucratis

Sais

Tanis (Zoan)

Pernefer

Solar cult-centre

LOWER
EGYPT

Merimdeh-ben-Salama

Bubastis
(Bast)

Tell-el-Yahudiyeh

Early capital of united Egypt

Giza

Heliopolis

Single state c. 3400

Libyan

MEMPHIS
Sakkara

SINAI

□ **Copper Mines**

Pyramids, 26th century

L.Mareotis

Fayum

Serabet-el-Khadem □ **Turquoise
Mines**

*Eastern
EGYPT*

Alphabet
c. 1500

MIDDLE

Desert

D

e

s

e

r

t

Tell-el-Amarna

Capital of Akhnaten, c. 1370 - 1352

Nile

Ptolemais

Founded by Ptolemy I (d. 282)

THEBES

Deir-el-Bahri

Karnak

Capital, early 2nd millennium

UPPER   EGYPT

Absorbed lower Egypt c. 3200

Ist Cataract

Horse, c.1900

Abu Simbel

Buhen

2nd Cataract

Nile

The Old Kingdom (c 2700-2180) was
the time of the Great Pyramid of
Cheops (c 2575). Middle Kingdom: c
2180. Then, after the Hyksos
(Asian) interlude, the New Kingdom
began in c 1570. Thothmes III
reigned in the 15th and Rameses II
in the 13th century.

0   100

Miles

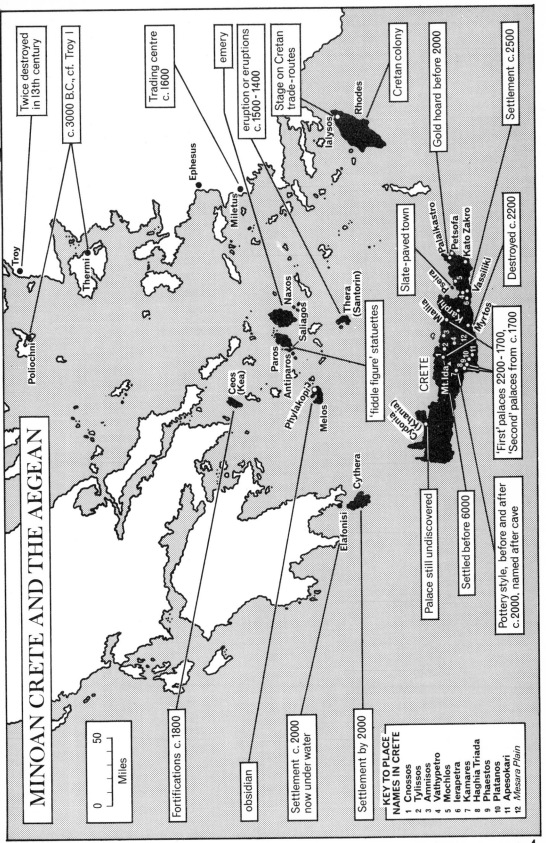

MINOAN CRETE AND THE AEGEAN

Twice destroyed in 13th century

c.3000 B.C., cf. Troy I

Trading centre c.1600

emery

eruption or eruptions c.1500-1400

Stage on Cretan trade-routes

Cretan colony

Gold hoard before 2000

Settlement c.2500

Destroyed c.2200

Troy

Poliochni

Thermi

Ephesus

Miletus

Naxos

Saliagos

Thera (Santorin)

Paros

Antiparos

Phylakopi

Melos

Ceos (Kea)

Ialysos

Rhodes

Palaikastro

Petsofa

Kato Zakro

Vassiliki

Psira

Mallia

Karphi

Myrtos

CRETE

Mt. Ida

Cydonia (Khania)

Slate-paved town

'fiddle figure' statuettes

Palace still undiscovered

Settled before 6000

Pottery style, before and after c.2000, named after cave

'First' palaces 2200-1700, 'Second' palaces from c.1700

Fortifications c.1800

obsidian

Settlement c.2000 now under water

Settlement by 2000

Cythera

Elafonisi

0   50

Miles

KEY TO PLACE NAMES IN CRETE

1 Cnossos
2 Tylissos
3 Amnisos
4 Vathypetro
5 Mochlos
6 Ierapetra
7 Kamares
8 Haghia Triada
9 Phaestos
10 Platanos
11 Apesokari
12 *Mesara Plain*

4

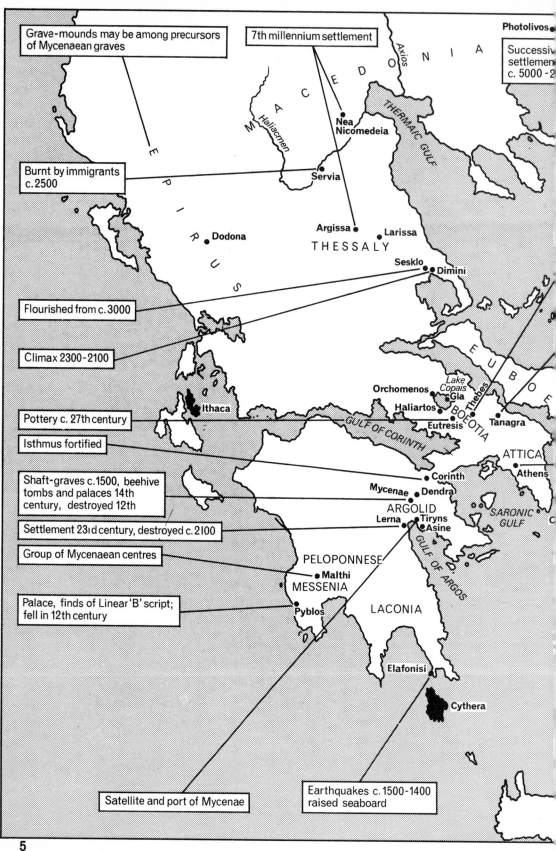

Grave-mounds may be among precursors of Mycenaean graves

7th millennium settlement

Photolivos

Successive settlement c. 5000 - 2

Nea Nicomedeia

THERMAIC GULF

Servia

Burnt by immigrants c. 2500

Axios

MACEDONIA

Haliacmen

EPIRUS

Dodona

Argissa

Larissa

THESSALY

Sesklo

Dimini

Flourished from c. 3000

Climax 2300 - 2100

Ithaca

Orchomenos

Lake Copais

Gla

Thebes

Haliartos

BOEOTIA

Eutresis

Tanagra

Pottery c. 27th century

GULF OF CORINTH

Isthmus fortified

EUBOE

ATTICA

Athens

Corinth

Shaft-graves c.1500, beehive tombs and palaces 14th century, destroyed 12th

Mycenae

Dendra

ARGOLID

Tiryns

SARONIC GULF

Lerna

Asine

Settlement 23rd century, destroyed c. 2100

PELOPONNESE

Group of Mycenaean centres

Malthi

MESSENIA

GULF OF ARGOS

LACONIA

Palace, finds of Linear 'B' script; fell in 12th century

Pyblos

Elafonisi

Cythera

Satellite and port of Mycenae

Earthquakes c. 1500-1400 raised seaboard

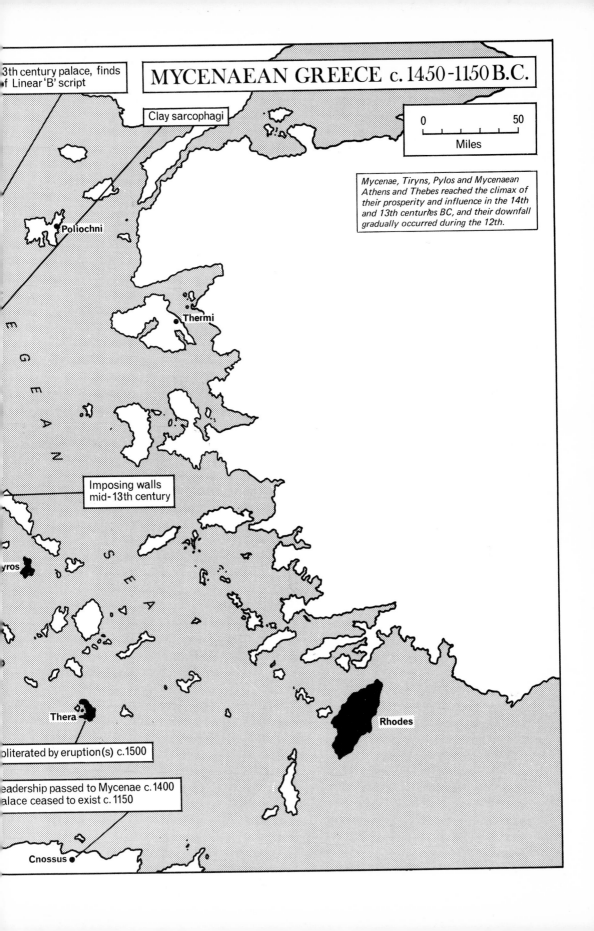

MYCENAEAN GREECE c. 1450-1150 B.C.

3th century palace, finds
f Linear 'B' script

Clay sarcophagi

0   50

Miles

Mycenae, Tiryns, Pylos and Mycenaean
Athens and Thebes reached the climax of
their prosperity and influence in the 14th
and 13th centuries BC, and their downfall
gradually occurred during the 12th.

Poliochni

Thermi

A
E
G
E
A
N

Imposing walls
mid-13th century

S
E
A

yros

Thera

Rhodes

bliterated by eruption(s) c.1500

eadership passed to Mycenae c.1400
alace ceased to exist c.1150

Cnossus

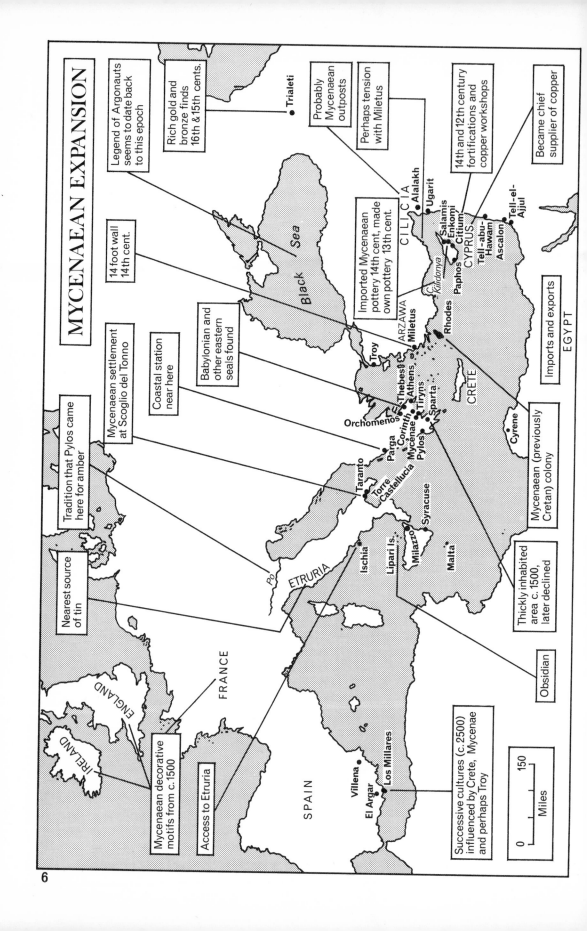

MYCENAEAN EXPANSION

Trialeti

Legend of Argonauts seems to date back to this epoch

Rich gold and bronze finds 16th & 15th cents.

Probably Mycenaean outposts

Perhaps tension with Miletus

14th and 12th century fortifications and copper workshops

Became chief supplier of copper

Imported Mycenaean pottery 14th cent, made own pottery 13th cent.

14 foot wall 14th cent.

Babylonian and other eastern seals found

Mycenaean settlement at Scoglio del Tonno

Coastal station near here

Tradition that Pylos came here for amber

Nearest source of tin

Mycenaean decorative motifs from c.1500

Access to Etruria

Successive cultures (c.2500) influenced by Crete, Mycenae and perhaps Troy

Thickly inhabited area c. 1500, later declined

Obsidian

Mycenaean (previously Cretan) colony

Imports and exports

Black Sea

CILICIA

Alalakh

Ugarit

Salamis
Enkomi
Citium
CYPRUS
Paphos
Tell-abu-Hawam
Ascalon
Tell-el-Ajiul

C. Kilidonya

ARZAWA

Rhodes

Miletus

Troy

Thebes
Athens
Orchomenos
Corinth
Mycenae
Tiryns
Pylos
Sparta

CRETE

Cyrene

Parga

Taranto

Torre
Castelluccia

Syracuse

Ischia

Lipari Is.

Milazzo

Malta

Po

ETRURIA

FRANCE

ENGLAND

IRELAND

SPAIN

Villena
El Argar
Los Millares

EGYPT

0   150
Miles

6

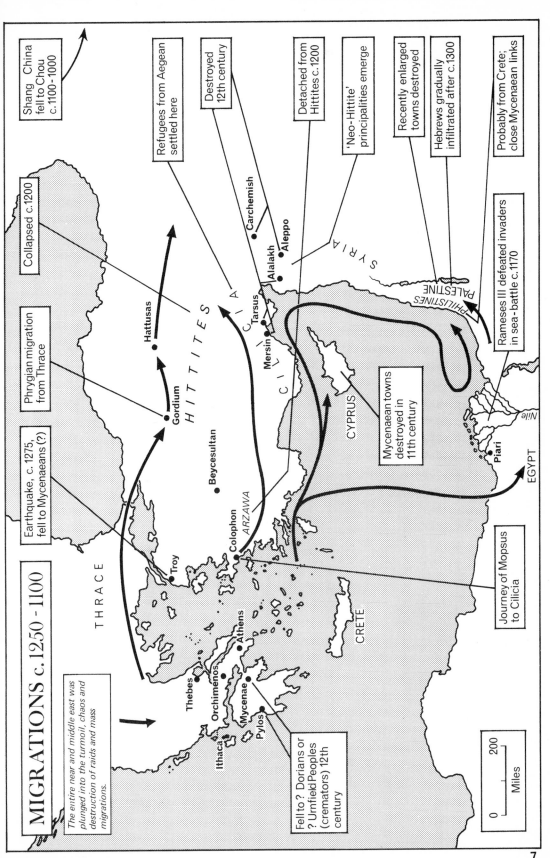

MIGRATIONS c. 1250 - 1100

The entire near and middle east was plunged into the turmoil, chaos and destruction of raids and mass migrations.

Shang China fell to Chou c. 1100-1000

Refugees from Aegean settled here

Destroyed 12th century

Detached from Hittites c. 1200

'Neo-Hittite' principalities emerge

Recently enlarged towns destroyed

Hebrews gradually infiltrated after c.1300

Probably from Crete; close Mycenaean links

Rameses III defeated invaders in sea-battle c. 1170

Collapsed c. 1200

Phrygian migration from Thrace

Earthquake, c. 1275, fell to Mycenaeans (?)

Mycenaean towns destroyed in 11th century

Journey of Mopsus to Cilicia

Fell to ? Dorians or ? Urnfield Peoples (cremators) 12th century

Carchemish

Aleppo

Alalakh

Tarsus

Hattusas

HITTITES

Mersin

CILICIA

Beycesultan

ARZAWA

Colophon

Troy

THRACE

Thebes

Orchimenos

Athens

Ithaca

Mycenae

Pylos

CRETE

CYPRUS

SYRIA

PALESTINE

PHILISTINES

Nile

Piari

EGYPT

0   200

Miles

7

B

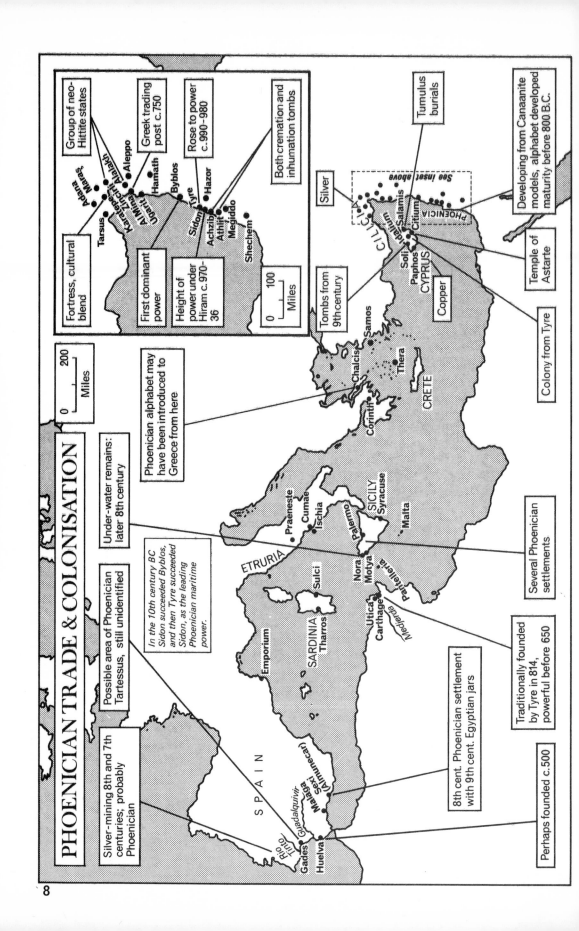

PHOENICIAN TRADE & COLONISATION

Silver-mining 8th and 7th centuries; probably Phoenician

Possible area of Phoenician Tartessus, still unidentified

Under-water remains: later 8th century

Phoenician alphabet may have been introduced to Greece from here

In the 10th century BC Sidon succeeded Byblos, and then Tyre succeeded Sidon, as the leading Phoenician maritime power.

Perhaps founded c.500

8th cent. Phoenician settlement with 9th cent. Egyptian jars

Traditionally founded by Tyre in 814, powerful before 650

Several Phoenician settlements

Colony from Tyre

Copper

Silver

Temple of Astarte

Developing from Canaanite models, alphabet developed maturity before 800 B.C.

Tumulus burials

Tombs from 9th century

Both cremation and inhumation tombs

Rose to power c..990–980

Greek trading post c.750

Group of neo-Hittite states

Fortress, cultural blend

First dominant power

Height of power under Hiram c. 970–36

SPAIN

Rio Tinto

Gades

Huelva

Guadalquivir

Malaga

Sexi (Almunecar)

SARDINIA

Tharros

Sulci

Emporium

ETRURIA

Praeneste

Cumae

Ischia

Palermo

Motya

Nora

Pantelleria

Medjerda

Utica

Carthage

SICILY

Syracuse

Malta

Samos

Chalcis

Corinth

Thera

CRETE

CYPRUS

Soli

Salamis

Paphos

Citium

Kition

PHOENICIA

CILICIA

See inset above

Tarsus

Adana

Mara

Karatepe

Zinjirli

Alalakh

Al Mina

Ugarit

Aleppo

Hamath

Byblos

Sidon

Tyre

Achzib

Athlit

Hazor

Megiddo

Shechem

Miles
0   200

Miles
0   100

8

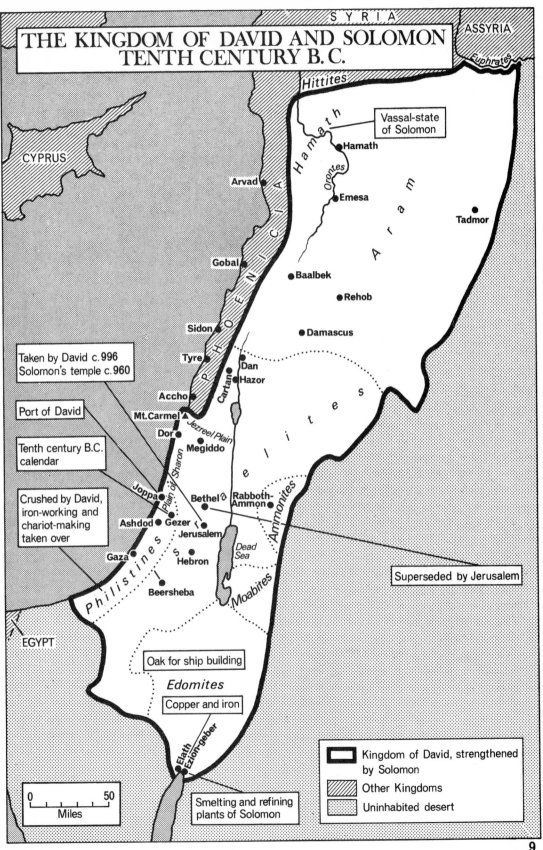

THE KINGDOM OF DAVID AND SOLOMON TENTH CENTURY B.C.

SYRIA

ASSYRIA

Euphrates

Hittites

CYPRUS

Hamath

Vassal-state of Solomon

●Hamath

Orontes

Arvad ●

●Emesa

Aram

●Tadmor

Gobal

●Baalbek

●Rehob

Sidon ●

●Damascus

Tyre ●

Taken by David c.996
Solomon's temple c.960

Cartan ●Dan
■Hazor

Accho ●

Port of David

Mt.Carmel ▲

Jezreel Plain

Dor ●

Israelites

Tenth century B.C.
calendar

Megiddo ●

Plain of Sharon

Joppa ●

Crushed by David,
iron-working and
chariot-making
taken over

Bethel ●

Rabboth-
Ammon ●

Ammonites

Ashdod ● Gezer ●

Jerusalem ●

Superseded by Jerusalem

Gaza ●

*Dead
Sea*

Hebron ●

Philistines

Beersheba ●

Moabites

EGYPT

Oak for ship building

Edomites

Copper and iron

Elath
Ezion-geber

Kingdom of David, strengthened
by Solomon

Other Kingdoms

Uninhabited desert

Smelting and refining
plants of Solomon

0   50
Miles

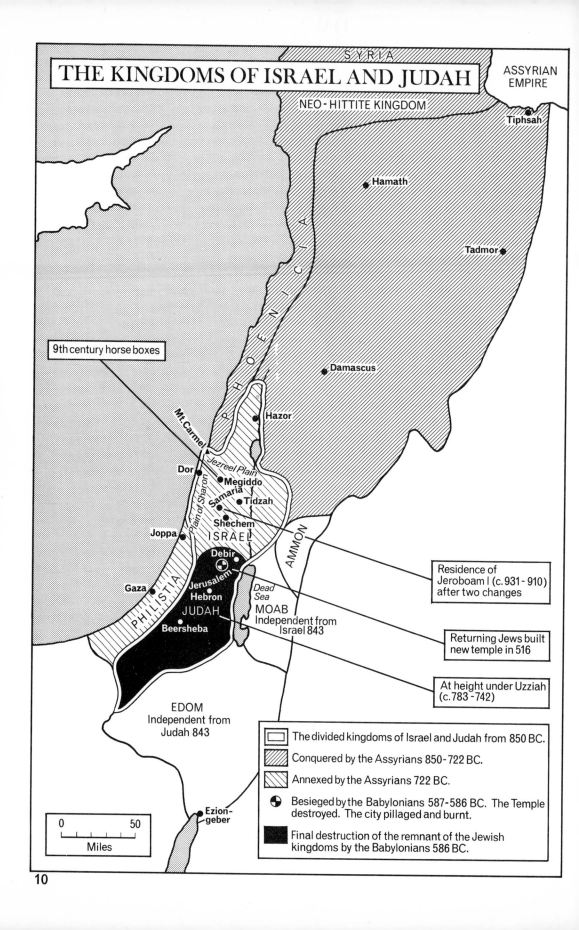

THE KINGDOMS OF ISRAEL AND JUDAH

SYRIA

ASSYRIAN EMPIRE

NEO-HITTITE KINGDOM

Tiphsah

Hamath

Tadmor

9th century horse boxes

P H O E N I C I A

Damascus

Mt. Carmel

Hazor

Jezreel Plain

Dor

Megiddo

Samaria

Tidzah

Plain of Sharon

Shechem

Joppa

ISRAEL

AMMON

Debir

Jerusalem

Gaza

Hebron

Dead Sea

Residence of Jeroboam I (c. 931-910) after two changes

Returning Jews built new temple in 516

At height under Uzziah (c. 783-742)

JUDAH

P H I L I S T I A

MOAB
Independent from
Israel 843

Beersheba

EDOM
Independent from
Judah 843

The divided kingdoms of Israel and Judah from 850 BC.

Conquered by the Assyrians 850-722 BC.

Annexed by the Assyrians 722 BC.

Besieged by the Babylonians 587-586 BC. The Temple destroyed. The city pillaged and burnt.

Final destruction of the remnant of the Jewish kingdoms by the Babylonians 586 BC.

Ezion-geber

0   50
Miles

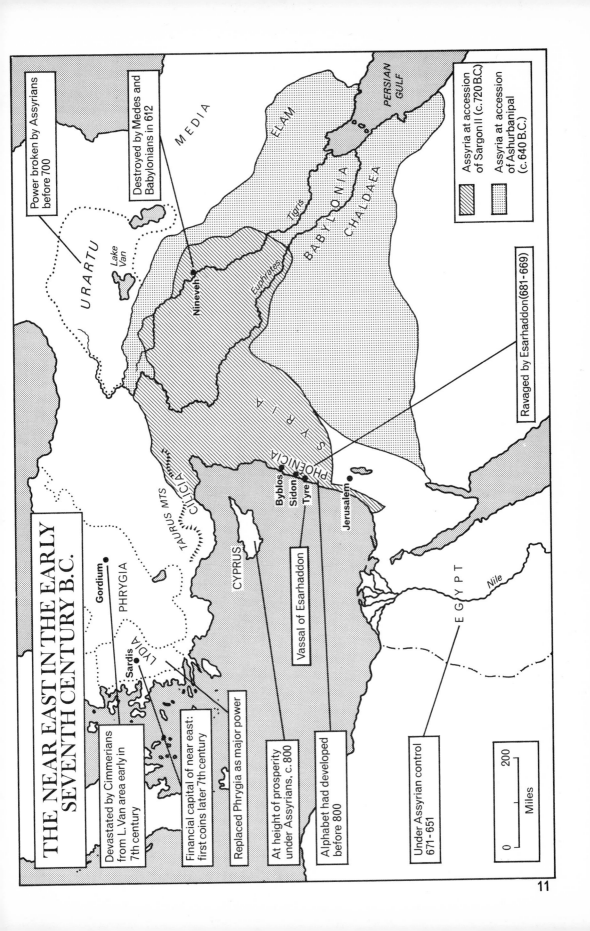

THE NEAR EAST IN THE EARLY SEVENTH CENTURY B.C.

MEDIA

ELAM

PERSIAN GULF

BABYLONIA

CHALDAEA

Tigris

Euphrates

URARTU

Lake Van

Nineveh

Power broken by Assyrians before 700

Destroyed by Medes and Babylonians in 612

Assyria at accession of Sargon II (c.720 B.C.)

Assyria at accession of Ashurbanipal (c. 640 B.C.)

Ravaged by Esarhaddon (681- 669)

S Y R I A

PHOENICIA

Byblos

Sidon

Tyre

Jerusalem

TAURUS MTS

CILICIA

CYPRUS

Gordium

PHRYGIA

Sardis

LYDIA

EGYPT

Nile

Devastated by Cimmerians from L. Van area early in 7th century

Financial capital of near east: first coins later 7th century

Replaced Phrygia as major power

At height of prosperity under Assyrians, c. 800

Alphabet had developed before 800

Vassal of Esarhaddon

Under Assyrian control 671- 651

0   200

Miles

11

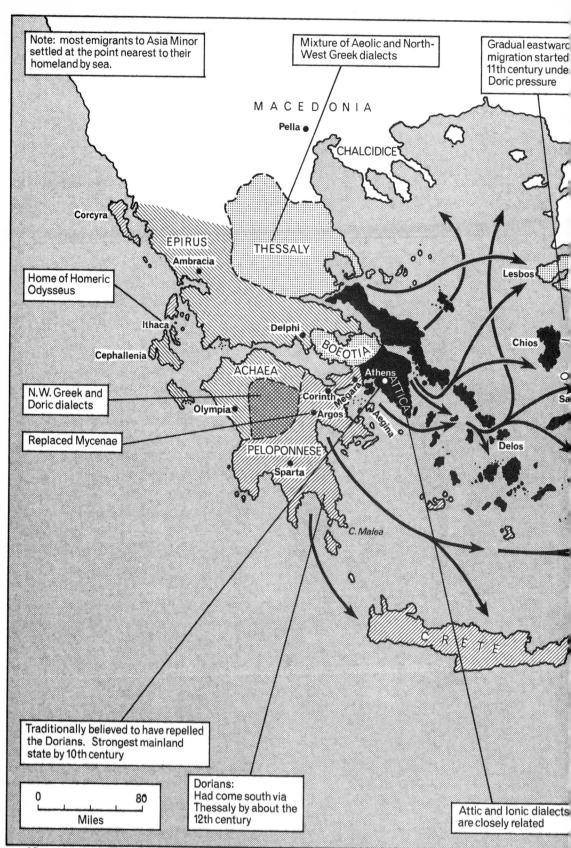

Note: most emigrants to Asia Minor settled at the point nearest to their homeland by sea.

Mixture of Aeolic and North-West Greek dialects

Gradual eastward migration started 11th century under Doric pressure

M A C E D O N I A

Pella ●

CHALCIDICE

Corcyra

EPIRUS

THESSALY

Ambracia

Home of Homeric Odysseus

Ithaca

Delphi

Lesbos

BOEOTIA

Chios

Cephallenia

ACHAEA

Athens

N.W. Greek and Doric dialects

Corinth

Megara

ATTICA

Sa

Olympia ●

Argos

Aegina

Replaced Mycenae

PELOPONNESE

Delos

Sparta

C. Malea

C R E T E

Traditionally believed to have repelled the Dorians. Strongest mainland state by 10th century

0 ———————— 80
Miles

Dorians: Had come south via Thessaly by about the 12th century

Attic and Ionic dialects are closely related

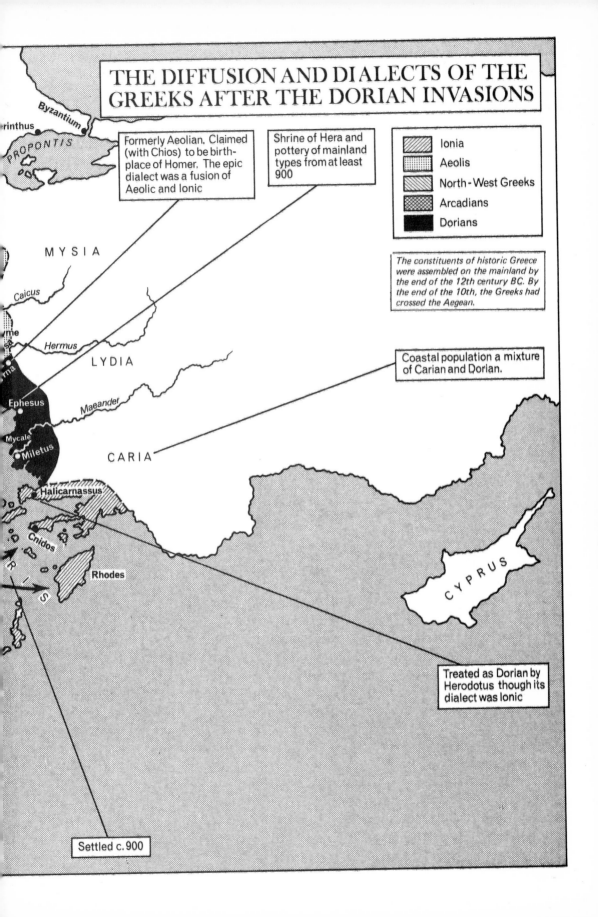

THE DIFFUSION AND DIALECTS OF THE GREEKS AFTER THE DORIAN INVASIONS

Formerly Aeolian. Claimed (with Chios) to be birthplace of Homer. The epic dialect was a fusion of Aeolic and Ionic

Shrine of Hera and pottery of mainland types from at least 900

▨	Ionia
▦	Aeolis
▧	North-West Greeks
▨	Arcadians
■	Dorians

The constituents of historic Greece were assembled on the mainland by the end of the 12th century BC. By the end of the 10th, the Greeks had crossed the Aegean.

Coastal population a mixture of Carian and Dorian.

Treated as Dorian by Herodotus though its dialect was Ionic

Settled c. 900

Byzantium
rinthus
PROPONTIS
MYSIA
Caicus
Hermus
LYDIA
rna
Ephesus
Mycale
Miletus
Maeander
CARIA
Halicarnassus
Cnidos
Rhodes
CYPRUS
R
I
S

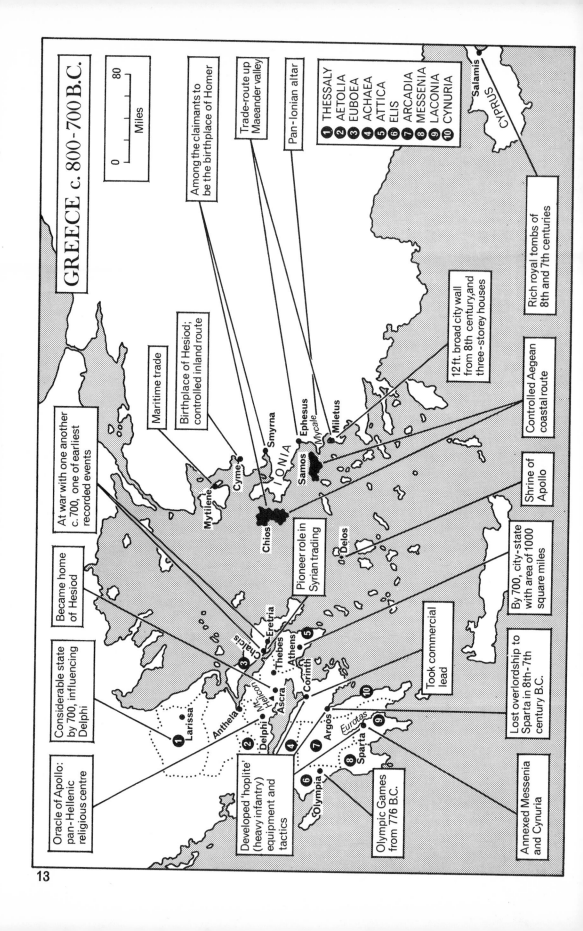

GREECE c. 800–700 B.C.

Miles
0   80

1 THESSALY
2 AETOLIA
3 EUBOEA
4 ACHAEA
5 ATTICA
6 ELIS
7 ARCADIA
8 MESSENIA
9 LACONIA
10 CYNURIA

Among the claimants to be the birthplace of Homer

Trade-route up Maeander valley

Pan-Ionian altar

Maritime trade

Birthplace of Hesiod; controlled inland route

At war with one another c. 700, one of earliest recorded events

Became home of Hesiod

Considerable state by 700, influencing Delphi

Oracle of Apollo: pan-Hellenic religious centre

12 ft. broad city wall from 8th century, and three-storey houses

Rich royal tombs of 8th and 7th centuries

Controlled Aegean coastal route

Pioneer role in Syrian trading

Shrine of Apollo

By 700, city-state with area of 1000 square miles

Took commercial lead

Lost overlordship to Sparta in 8th–7th century B.C.

Developed 'hoplite' (heavy infantry) equipment and tactics

Olympic Games from 776 B.C.

Annexed Messenia and Cynuria

CYPRUS

Salamis

Smyrna
Cyme
Mytilene
IONIA
Ephesus
Mycale
Samos
Miletus
Chios
Delos

Eretria
Chalcis
Thebes
Athens
Corinth
Larissa
Anthela
Delphi
Mt.Helicon
Ascra
Argos
Eurotas
Sparta
Olympia

1 Larissa
2 Delphi
3 Chalcis
4
5 Athens
6 Olympia
7
8 Sparta
9
10 Argos

13

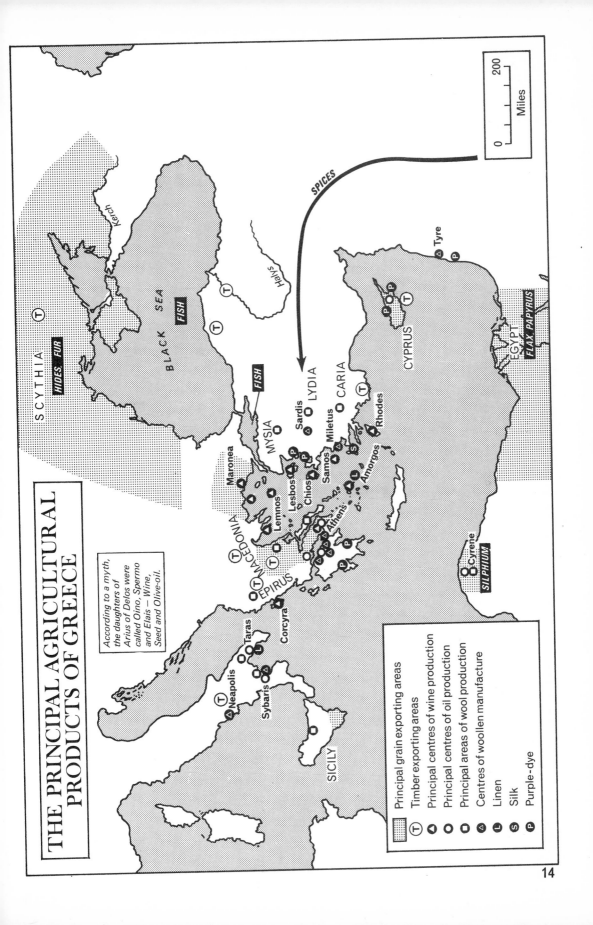

THE PRINCIPAL AGRICULTURAL PRODUCTS OF GREECE

According to a myth, the daughters of Arius of Delos were called Oino, Spermo and Elais — Wine, Seed and Olive-oil.

Legend:

	Principal grain exporting areas
	Timber exporting areas
◐	Principal centres of wine production
○	Principal centres of oil production
▢	Principal areas of wool production
◭	Centres of woollen manufacture
Ⓛ	Linen
Ⓢ	Silk
Ⓟ	Purple-dye

SCYTHIA: HIDES: FUR

BLACK SEA

FISH

Kerch

Halys

SPICES

Tyre

CYPRUS

EGYPT FLAX PAPYRUS

Sardis

LYDIA

CARIA

Miletus

Rhodes

Samos

Amorgos

MYSIA

Maronea

Lesbos

Chios

Lemnos

MACEDONIA

Athens

EPIRUS

Corcyra

Taras

Neapolis

Sybaris

SICILY

Cyrene

SILPHIUM

0   200
Miles

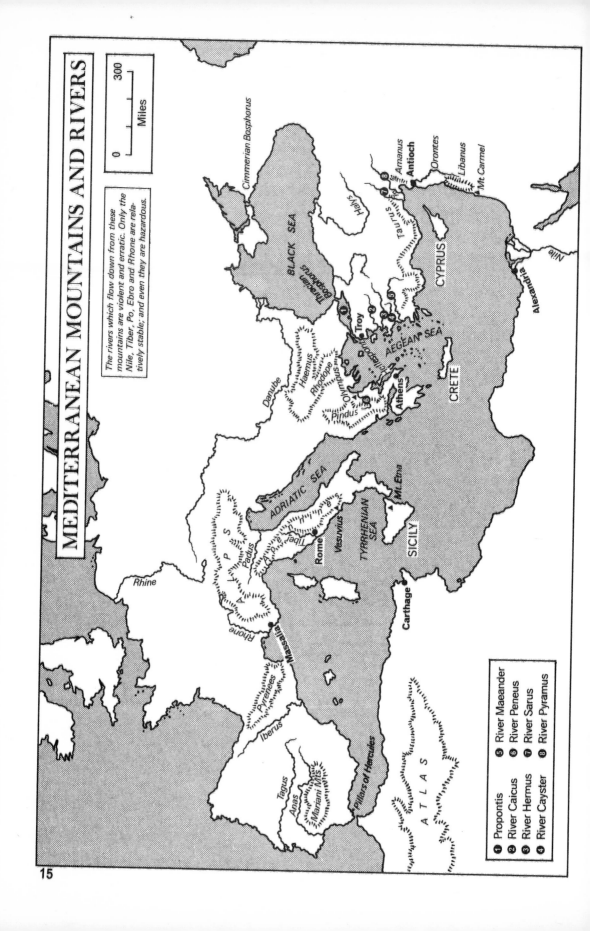

MEDITERRANEAN MOUNTAINS AND RIVERS

The rivers which flow down from these mountains are violent and erratic. Only the Nile, Tiber, Po, Ebro and Rhone are relatively stable; and even they are hazardous.

1 Propontis
2 River Caicus
3 River Hermus
4 River Cayster
5 River Maeander
6 River Peneus
7 River Sarus
8 River Pyramus

0 ⌐ 300
Miles

15

RAINFALL IN THE MEDITERRANEAN AREA

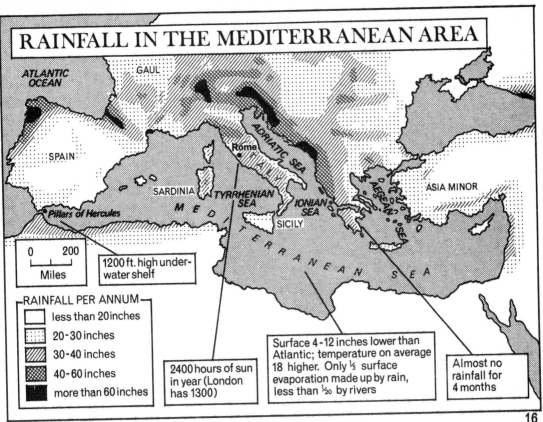

ATLANTIC OCEAN

GAUL

SPAIN

Pillars of Hercules

SARDINIA

Rome

ADRIATIC SEA

ITALY

TYRRHENIAN SEA

SICILY

IONIAN SEA

AEGEAN SEA

ASIA MINOR

MEDITERRANEAN SEA

0   200
Miles

1200 ft. high under-water shelf

RAINFALL PER ANNUM
- less than 20 inches
- 20-30 inches
- 30-40 inches
- 40-60 inches
- more than 60 inches

2400 hours of sun in year (London has 1300)

Surface 4-12 inches lower than Atlantic; temperature on average 18 higher. Only ⅓ surface evaporation made up by rain, less than ¹⁄₂₀ by rivers

Almost no rainfall for 4 months

16

MINERALS IN THE EASTERN MEDITERRANEAN AREA

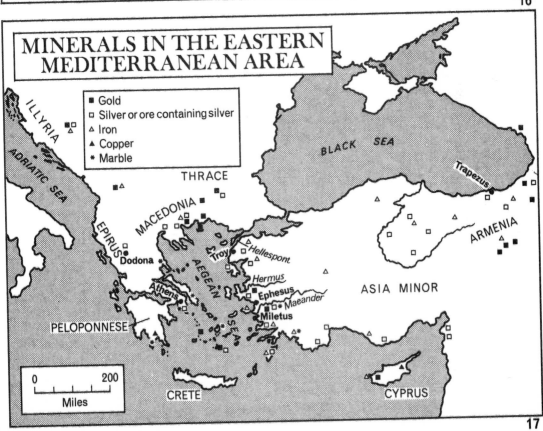

- ■ Gold
- □ Silver or ore containing silver
- △ Iron
- ▲ Copper
- ✳ Marble

ILLYRIA

ADRIATIC SEA

EPIRUS

Dodona

MACEDONIA

THRACE

BLACK SEA

Trapezus

Troy

Hellespont

Hermus

ARMENIA

Athens

AEGEAN SEA

Ephesus

Maeander

Miletus

ASIA MINOR

PELOPONNESE

0   200
Miles

CRETE

CYPRUS

17

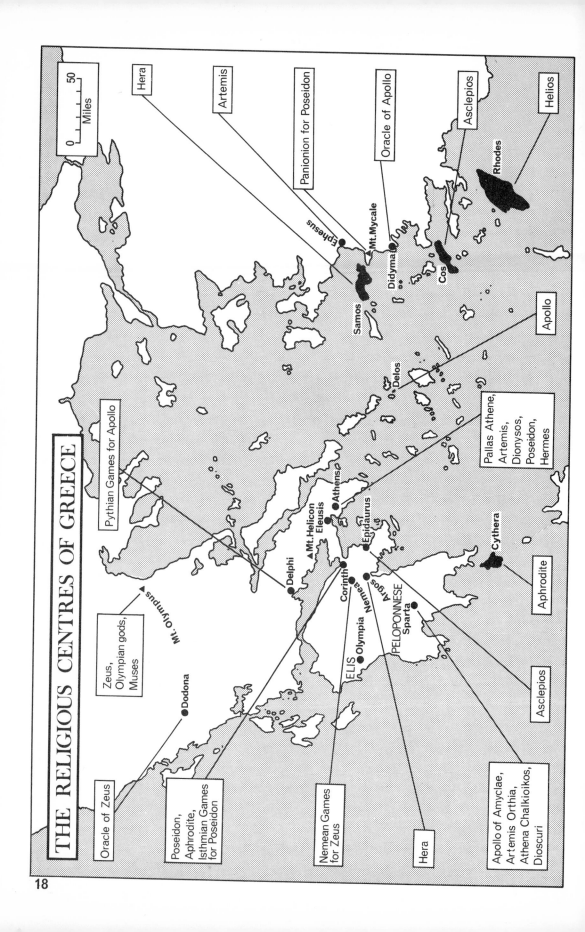

THE RELIGIOUS CENTRES OF GREECE

Oracle of Zeus

Zeus, Olympian gods, Muses

Poseidon, Aphrodite, Isthmian Games for Poseidon

Pythian Games for Apollo

Nemean Games for Zeus

Hera

Apollo of Amyclae, Artemis Orthia, Athena Chalkioikos, Dioscuri

Hera

Artemis

Panionion for Poseidon

Oracle of Apollo

Asclepios

Helios

Apollo

Pallas Athene, Artemis, Dionysos, Poseidon, Hermes

Aphrodite

Asclepios

Mt. Olympus

Dodona

Delphi

Mt. Helicon
Eleusis

Athens

Epidaurus

Corinth

Nemea

Argos

ELIS

Olympia

PELOPONNESE
Sparta

Cythera

Delos

Ephesus

Mt. Mycale

Didyma

Cos

Samos

Rhodes

Miles
0   50

18

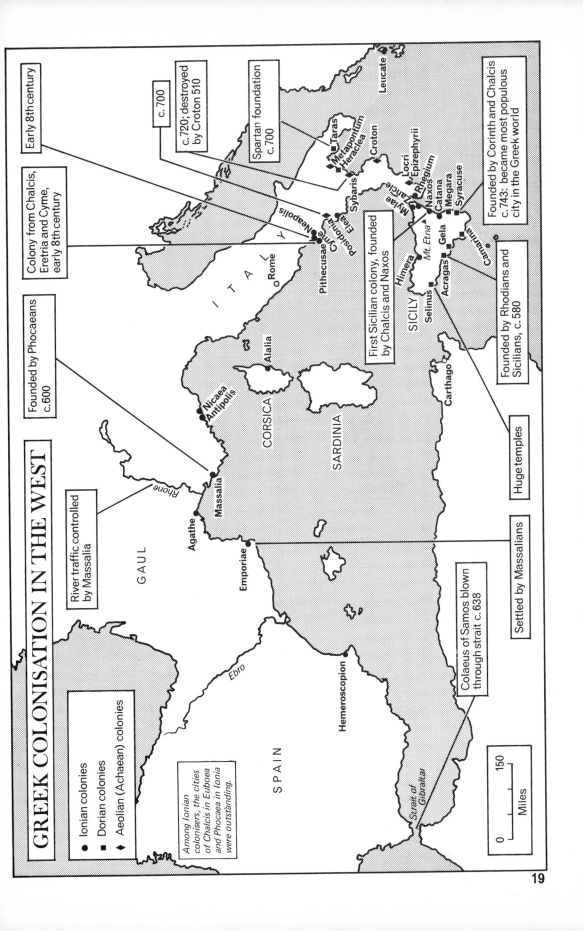

GREEK COLONISATION IN THE WEST

- • Ionian colonies
- ■ Dorian colonies
- ◆ Aeolian (Achaean) colonies

Among Ionian colonisers, the cities of Chalcis in Euboea and Phocaea in Ionia were outstanding.

Early 8th century

c. 700

c. 720; destroyed by Croton 510

Spartan foundation c. 700

Founded by Corinth and Chalcis c. 743: became most populous city in the Greek world

Colony from Chalcis, Eretria and Cyme, early 8th century

First Sicilian colony, founded by Chalcis and Naxos

Founded by Rhodians and Sicilians, c. 580

Huge temples

Founded by Phocaeans c. 600

River traffic controlled by Massalia

Settled by Massalians

Colaeus of Samos blown through strait c. 638

Place labels: Leucate, Taras, Metapontum, Heraclea, Croton, Locri, Epizephyrii, Rhegium, Naxos, Catana, Megara, Syracuse, Mylae, Zancle, Sybaris, Elea, Posidonia, Neapolis, Cyme, Pithecusae, Rome, Himera, Selinus, Acragas, Gela, Camarina, Mt. Etna, SICILY, Carthago, ITALY, Alalia, CORSICA, SARDINIA, Nicaea, Antipolis, Massalia, Agathe, Emporiae, GAUL, Rhone, Ebro, Hemeroscopion, SPAIN, Strait of Gibraltar

0 150
Miles

19

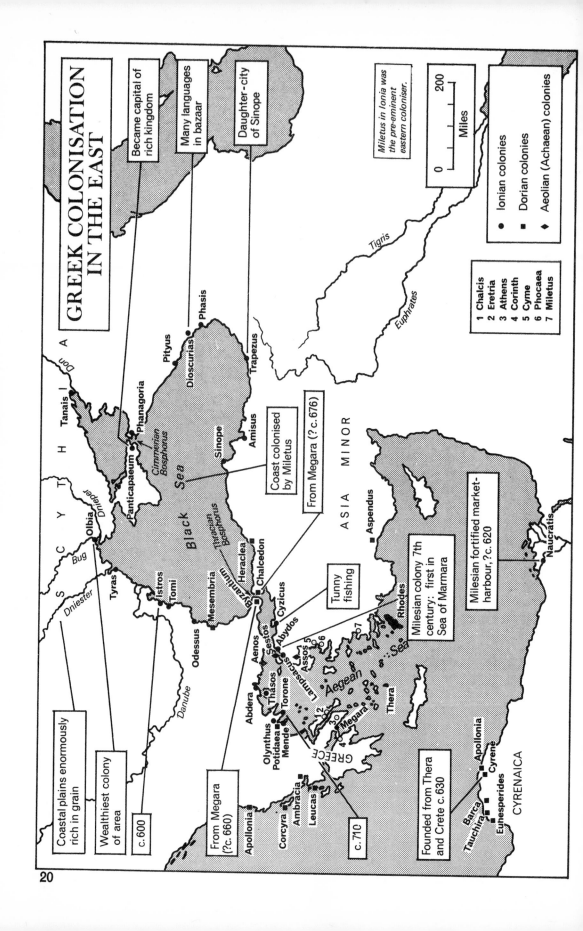

GREEK COLONISATION IN THE EAST

Became capital of rich kingdom

Many languages in bazaar

Daughter-city of Sinope

Miletus in Ionia was the pre-eminent eastern coloniser.

0   200
Miles

● Ionian colonies
■ Dorian colonies
◆ Aeolian (Achaean) colonies

1 Chalcis
2 Eretria
3 Athens
4 Corinth
5 Cyme
6 Phocaea
7 Miletus

Tigris

Euphrates

Don

Tanais I

S C Y T H I A

Dnieper

Phanagoria

Cimmerian Bosphorus

Panticapaeum

Olbia

Bug

Dniester

Tyras

Istros

Tomi

Mesembria

Thracian Bosphorus

Heraclea

Byzantium

Chalcedon

Odessus

Danube

Cyzicus

Abydos

Sestos

Aenos

Lampsacus

Assos

Thasos

Torone

Abdera

Olynthus

Potidaea

Mende

Megara

Thera

Phasis

Pityus

Dioscurias

Trapezus

Amisus

Sinope

Black Sea

A S I A   M I N O R

Aspendus

Rhodes

Aegean Sea

GREECE

Naucratis

Coast colonised by Miletus

From Megara (?c. 676)

Tunny fishing

Milesian colony 7th century: first in Sea of Marmara

Milesian fortified market-harbour, ?c. 620

Coastal plains enormously rich in grain

Wealthiest colony of area

c. 600

From Megara (?c. 660)

c. 710

Founded from Thera and Crete c. 630

Apollonia

Corcyra

Ambracia

Leucas

Apollonia

Cyrene

Barca

Tauchira

Eunesperides

CYRENAICA

20

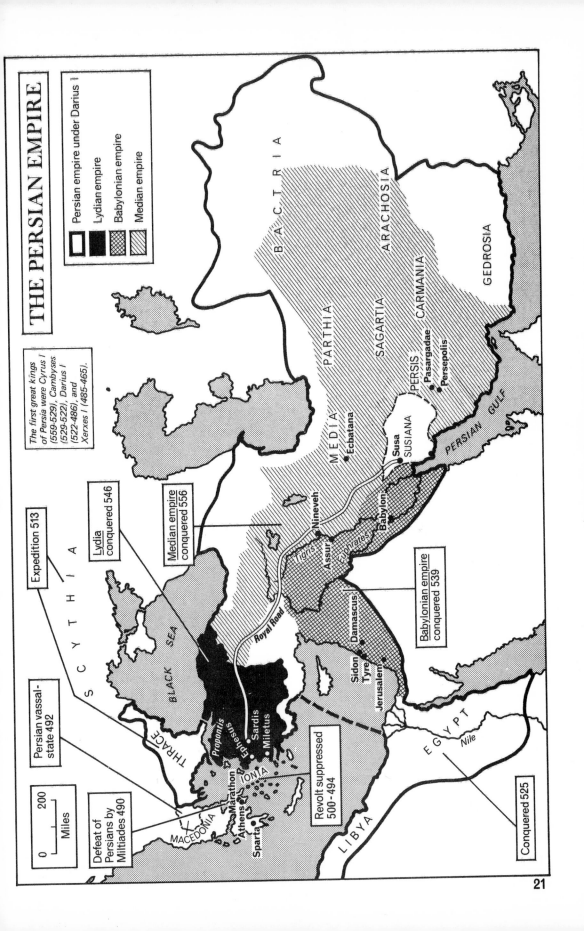

THE PERSIAN EMPIRE

Persian empire under Darius I

Lydian empire

Babylonian empire

Median empire

The first great kings of Persia were Cyrus I (559-529), Cambyses (529-522), Darius I (522-486), and Xerxes I (485-465).

Expedition 513

Persian vassal-state 492

Defeat of Persians by Miltiades 490

Lydia conquered 546

Median empire conquered 556

Babylonian empire conquered 539

Revolt suppressed 500 - 494

Conquered 525

0   200

Miles

SCYTHIA

THRACE

BLACK SEA

MACEDONIA

Athens

Sparta

Marathon

Propontis

Ephesus

Sardis

Miletus

IONIA

Assur

Nineveh

Tigris

Euphrates

Babylon

Royal Road

Damascus

Sidon

Tyre

Jerusalem

EGYPT

Nile

LIBYA

MEDIA

Ecbatana

Susa

SUSIANA

PARTHIA

SAGARTIA

PERSIS

Pasargadae

Persepolis

CARMANIA

ARACHOSIA

BACTRIA

GEDROSIA

PERSIAN GULF

21

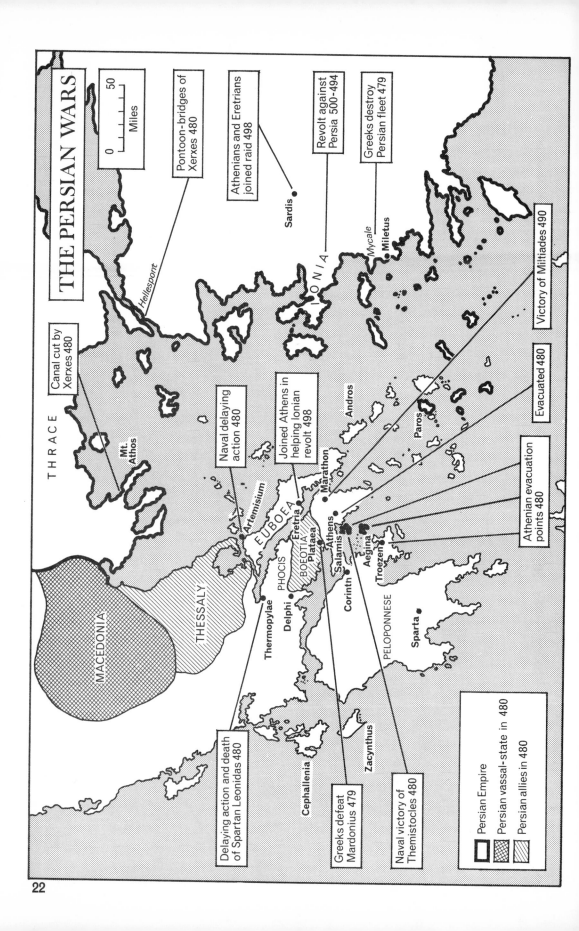

THE PERSIAN WARS

0 50
Miles

Pontoon-bridges of Xerxes 480

Athenians and Eretrians joined raid 498

Revolt against Persia 500-494

Greeks destroy Persian fleet 479

Canal cut by Xerxes 480

Naval delaying action 480

Joined Athens in helping Ionian revolt 498

Delaying action and death of Spartan Leonidas 480

Greeks defeat Mardonius 479

Naval victory of Themistocles 480

Evacuated 480

Victory of Miltiades 490

Athenian evacuation points 480

Sardis

Mycale

Miletus

IONIA

THRACE

Hellespont

Mt. Athos

MACEDONIA

THESSALY

PHOCIS

Delphi

Thermopylae

Artemisium

EUBOEA

Eretria

BOEOTIA

Plataea

Marathon

Athens

Salamis

Aegina

Troezen

Corinth

PELOPONNESE

Sparta

Andros

Paros

Zacynthus

Cephallenia

Persian Empire

Persian vassal-state in 480

Persian allies in 480

22

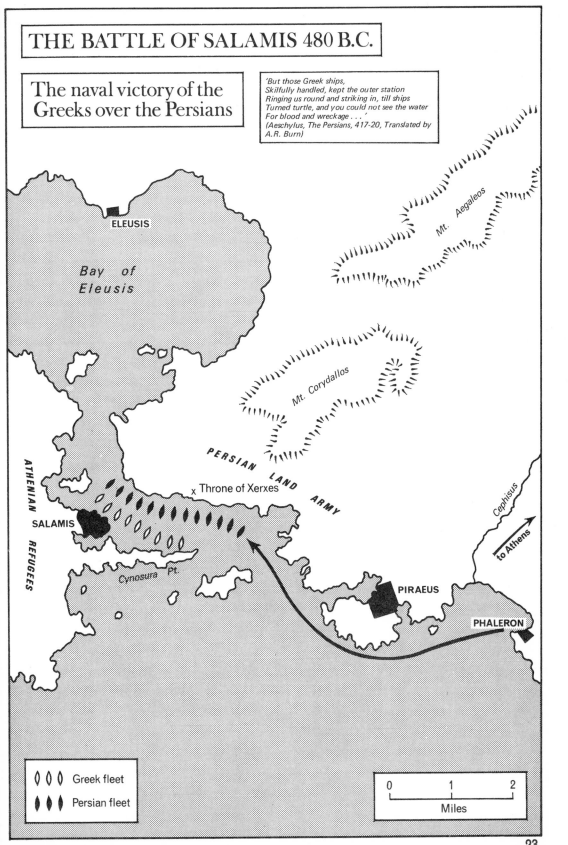

THE BATTLE OF SALAMIS 480 B.C.

The naval victory of the Greeks over the Persians

'But those Greek ships,
Skilfully handled, kept the outer station
Ringing us round and striking in, till ships
Turned turtle, and you could not see the water
For blood and wreckage . . .'
(Aeschylus, The Persians, 417-20, Translated by A.R. Burn)

ELEUSIS

Bay of Eleusis

Mt. Aegaleos

Mt. Corydallos

PERSIAN LAND ARMY

x Throne of Xerxes

Cephisus

to Athens

SALAMIS

ATHENIAN REFUGEES

Cynosura Pt.

PIRAEUS

PHALERON

◊ ◊ ◊ Greek fleet
◆ ◆ ◆ Persian fleet

0   1   2
Miles

23

C

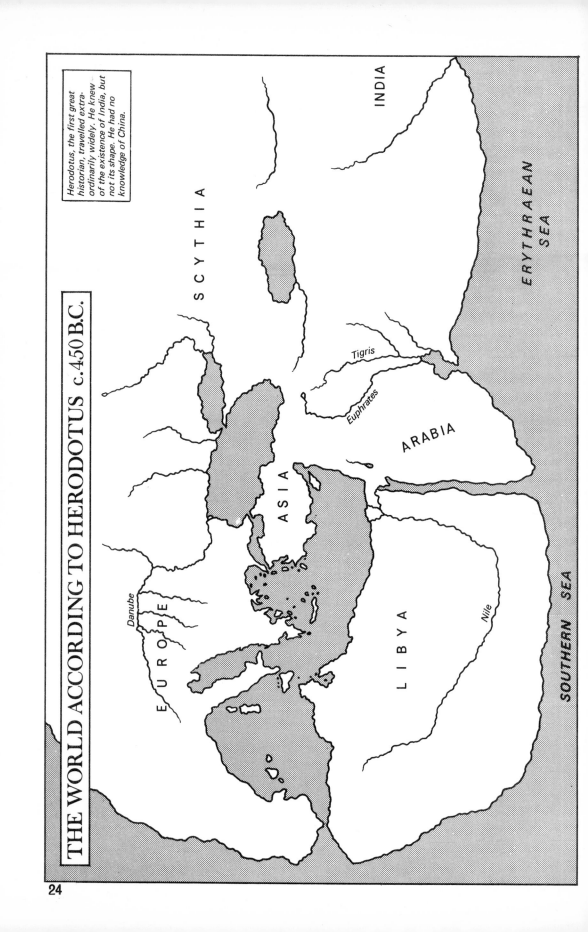

THE WORLD ACCORDING TO HERODOTUS c.450 B.C.

Herodotus, the first great historian, travelled extraordinarily widely. He knew of the existence of India, but not its shape. He had no knowledge of China.

INDIA

SCYTHIA

ERYTHRAEAN SEA

Tigris

Euphrates

ARABIA

ASIA

EUROPE

Danube

LIBYA

Nile

SOUTHERN SEA

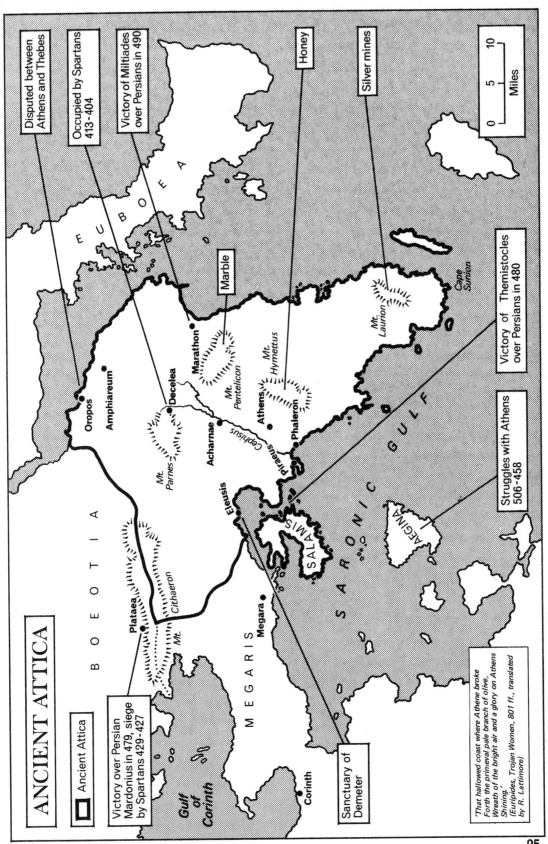

ANCIENT ATTICA

□ Ancient Attica

Disputed between Athens and Thebes

Occupied by Spartans 413-404

Victory of Miltiades over Persians in 490

Marble

Honey

Silver mines

Victory of Themistocles over Persians in 480

Struggles with Athens 506-458

Victory over Persian Mardonius in 479, siege by Spartans 429-427

Sanctuary of Demeter

0 5 10
Miles

EUBOEA

Oropos

Amphiareum

Decelea

Marathon

Mt. Parnes

Mt. Pentelicon

Acharnae

Cephisus

Athens

Mt. Hymettus

Phaleron

Piraeus

Mt. Laurion

Cape Sunion

SARONIC GULF

Eleusis

SALAMIS

AEGINA

Plataea

Mt. Cithaeron

Megara

MEGARIS

Corinth

Gulf of Corinth

BOEOTIA

'That hallowed coast where Athene broke
Forth the primeval pale branch of olive,
Wreath of the bright air and a glory on Athens
Shining.'
(Euripides, Trojan Women, 801 ff., translated
by R. Lattimore)

25

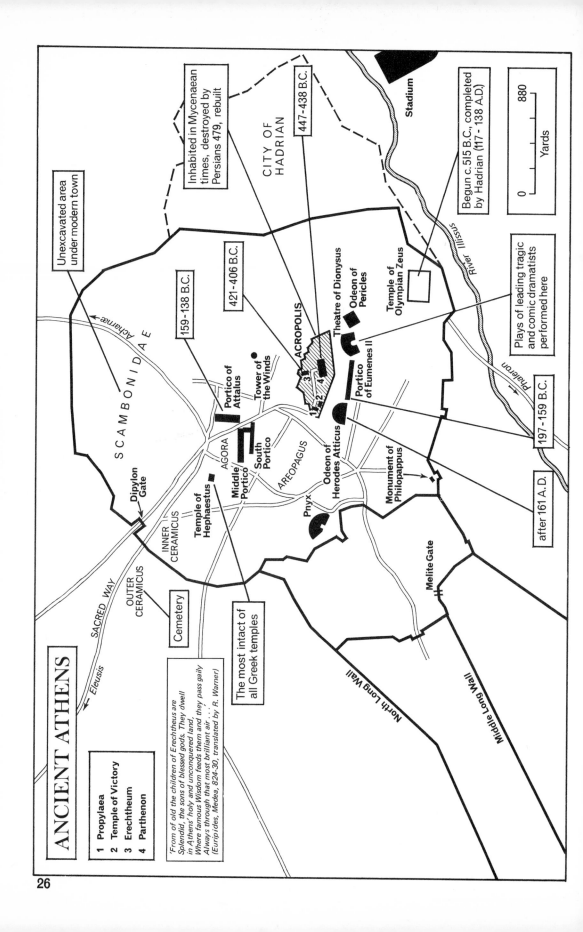

ANCIENT ATHENS

1 Propylaea
2 Temple of Victory
3 Erechtheum
4 Parthenon

'From of old the children of Erechtheus are
Splendid, the sons of blessed gods. They dwell
In Athens' holy and unconquered land,
Where famous Wisdom feeds them and they pass gaily
Always through that most brilliant air . . .'.
(Euripides, Medea, 824-30, translated by R. Warner)

Cemetery

The most intact of
all Greek temples

Unexcavated area
under modern town

Inhabited in Mycenaean
times, destroyed by
Persians 479, rebuilt

447 - 438 B.C.

421 - 406 B.C.

159 - 138 B.C.

Begun c.515 B.C., completed
by Hadrian (117 - 138 A.D.)

Plays of leading tragic
and comic dramatists
performed here

197 - 159 B.C.

after 161 A.D.

0   880

Yards

CITY OF
HADRIAN

Stadium

River Illissus

Phaleron

ACROPOLIS

Theatre of Dionysus

Odeon of
Pericles

Temple of
Olympian Zeus

Portico of Eumenes II

Odeon of
Herodes Atticus

Monument of
Philopappus

AREOPAGUS

Pnyx

Temple of Hephaestus

Middle
Portico

South
Portico

AGORA

Portico of
Attalus

Tower of
the Winds

S C A M B O N I D A E

Acharnae

Dipylon
Gate

INNER
CERAMICUS

OUTER
CERAMICUS

SACRED WAY

Eleusis

Melite Gate

North Long Wall

Middle Long Wall

26

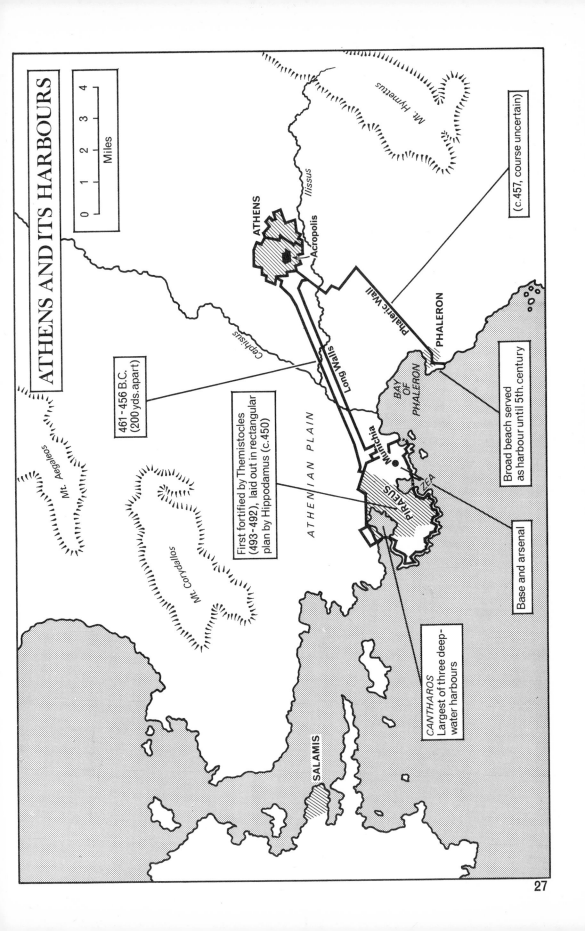

ATHENS AND ITS HARBOURS

Miles
0 1 2 3 4

Mt. Aegaleos

Mt. Corydallos

Cephisus

ATHENS

Acropolis

Ilissus

Mt. Hymettus

ATHENIAN PLAIN

Long Walls

Phaleric Wall

(c.457, course uncertain)

PHALERON

BAY OF PHALERON

461 - 456 B.C. (200 yds. apart)

First fortified by Themistocles (493-492), laid out in rectangular plan by Hippodamus (c.450)

Munichia

PIRAEUS

ZEA

Broad beach served as harbour until 5th. century

Base and arsenal

CANTHAROS Largest of three deep-water harbours

SALAMIS

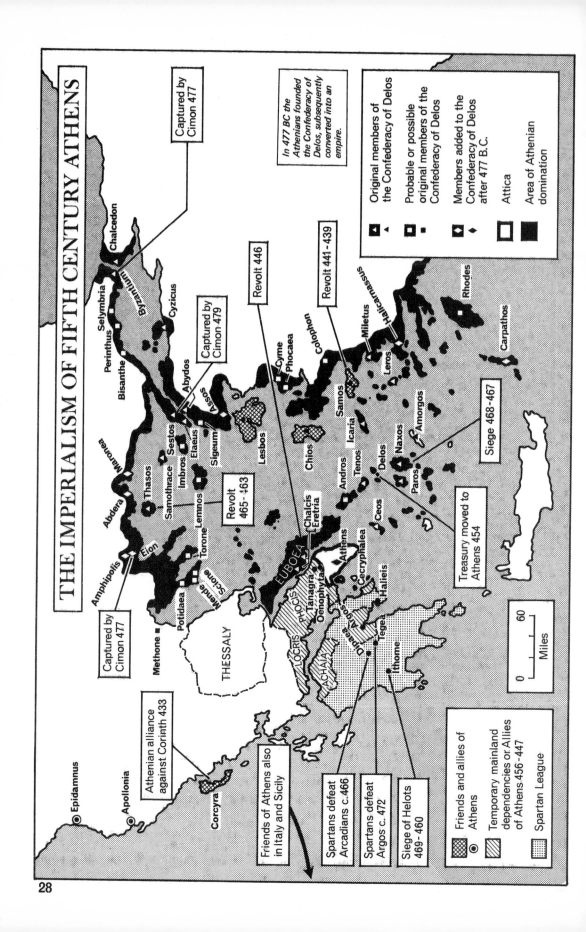

THE IMPERIALISM OF FIFTH CENTURY ATHENS

In 477 BC the Athenians founded the Confederacy of Delos, subsequently converted into an empire.

- ◄ Original members of the Confederacy of Delos
- ■ Probable or possible original members of the Confederacy of Delos
- ♦ Members added to the Confederacy of Delos after 477 B.C.
- ☐ Attica
- ■ Area of Athenian domination

Captured by Cimon 477

Captured by Cimon 479

Revolt 446

Revolt 441-439

Revolt 465-463

Siege 468-467

Treasury moved to Athens 454

Captured by Cimon 477

Athenian alliance against Corinth 433

Friends of Athens also in Italy and Sicily

Spartans defeat Arcadians c.466

Spartans defeat Argos c. 472

Siege of Helots 469-460

- ⊚ Friends and allies of Athens
- Temporary mainland dependencies or Allies of Athens 456-447
- Spartan League

0   60
Miles

Epidamnus

Apollonia

Corcyra

THESSALY

Methone ■

Amphipolis

Eion

Potidaea

Mende

Scione

Torone

Abdera

Maronea

Thasos

Samothrace

Imbros

Lemnos

Sestos

Elaeus

Sigeum

Assos

Abydos

Perinthus

Selymbria

Bisanthe

Byzantium

Chalcedon

Cyzicus

Maenus

Lesbos

Chios

Cyme

Phocaea

Colophon

Miletus

Halicarnassus

Samos

Icaria

Leros

Rhodes

Carpathos

Andros

Tenos

Naxos

Amorgos

Paros

Delos

Ceos

Cecryphalea

Athens

EUBOEA

Chalcis

Eretria

Tanagra

Oenophyta

PHOCIS

LOCRIS

ACHAIA

Aegina

Halieis

Tegea

Ithome

Argos

28

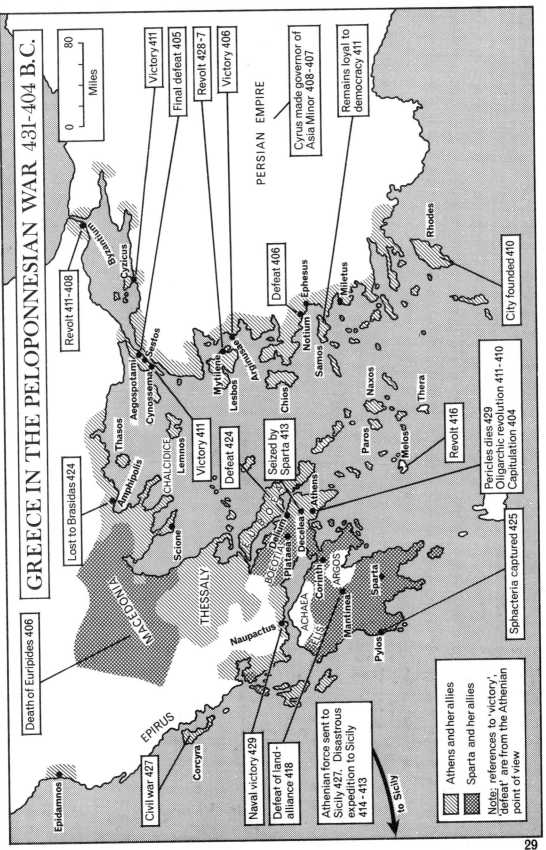

GREECE IN THE PELOPONNESIAN WAR 431–404 B.C.

0   80
Miles

Victory 411

Final defeat 405

Revolt 428–7

Victory 406

Cyrus made governor of Asia Minor 408–407

Remains loyal to democracy 411

PERSIAN EMPIRE

Revolt 411–408

Byzantium

Cyzicus

Rhodes

Defeat 406

Ephesus

Miletus

Sestos

Aegospotami

Cynossema

Mytilene

Arginussae

Notium

Samos

Lesbos

Chios

Thasos

CHALCIDICE

Lemnos

Victory 411

Defeat 424

Naxos

Paros

Thera

Revolt 416

City founded 410

Melos

Seized by Sparta 413

Amphipolis

Scione

Lost to Brasidas 424

MACEDONIA

THESSALY

BOEOTIA

Delium

Plataea

Decelea

Athens

Corinth

ARGOS

Mantinea

Sparta

ACHAEA

ELIS

Naupactus

Pericles dies 429
Oligarchic revolution 411–410
Capitulation 404

Sphacteria captured 425

Pylos

Death of Euripides 406

EPIRUS

Corcyra

Civil war 427

Naval victory 429

Defeat of land-alliance 418

Athenian force sent to Sicily 427. Disastrous expedition to Sicily 414–413

to Sicily

Epidamnos

Athens and her allies

Sparta and her allies

Note: references to 'victory',
'defeat' are from the Athenian
point of view

29

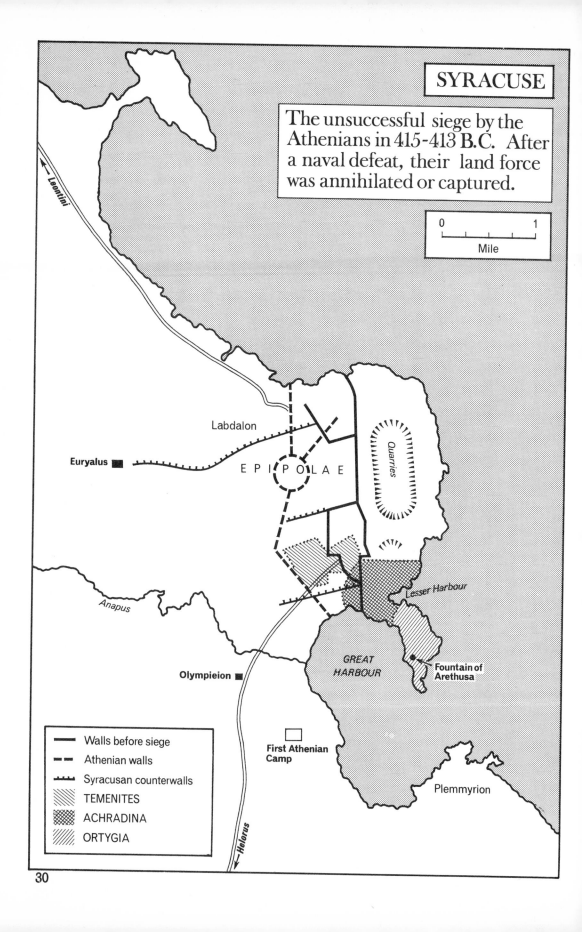

SYRACUSE

The unsuccessful siege by the Athenians in 415-413 B.C. After a naval defeat, their land force was annihilated or captured.

0   1
Mile

Leontini

Labdalon

Euryalus

E P I P O L A E

Quarries

Anapus

Lesser Harbour

Olympieion

GREAT HARBOUR

Fountain of Arethusa

First Athenian Camp

Plemmyrion

Walls before siege
Athenian walls
Syracusan counterwalls
TEMENITES
ACHRADINA
ORTYGIA

Helorus

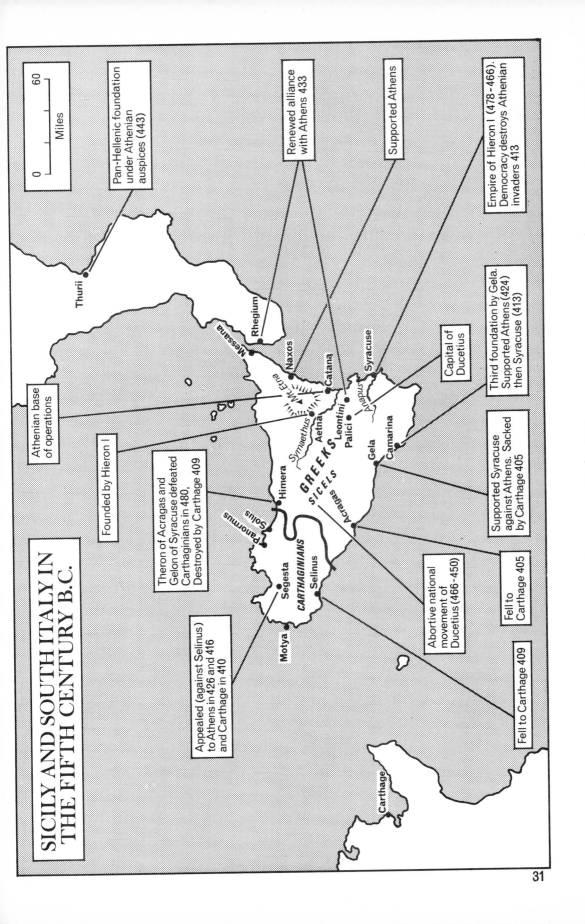

SICILY AND SOUTH ITALY IN THE FIFTH CENTURY B.C.

Miles
0   60

Pan-Hellenic foundation under Athenian auspices (443)

Renewed alliance with Athens 433

Supported Athens

Empire of Hieron I (478 - 466). Democracy destroys Athenian invaders 413

Athenian base of operations

Founded by Hieron I

Theron of Acragas and Gelon of Syracuse defeated Carthaginians in 480, Destroyed by Carthage 409

Capital of Ducetius

Third foundation by Gela. Supported Athens then Syracuse (413)

Supported Syracuse against Athens. Sacked by Carthage 405

Fell to Carthage 405

Appealed (against Selinus) to Athens in 426 and 416 and Carthage in 410

Abortive national movement of Ducetius (466 - 450)

Fell to Carthage 409

Thurii

Rhegium

Messana

Naxos

Catana

Syracuse

M. Etna

Symaethus

Aetna

Leontini

Palici

Anapus

GREEKS

SICELS

Gela

Camarina

Himera

Acragas

Solus

Panormus

CARTHAGINIANS

Segesta

Selinus

Motya

Carthage

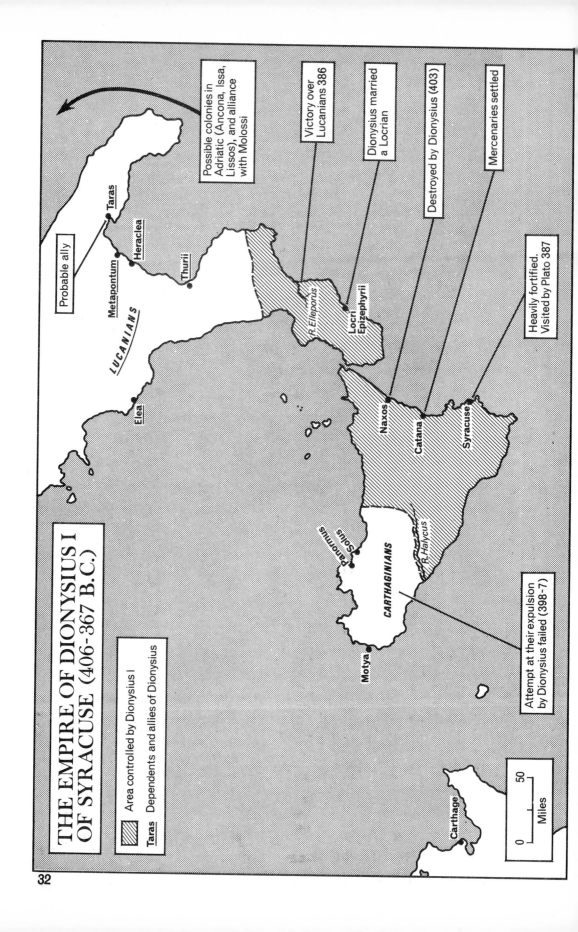

THE EMPIRE OF DIONYSIUS I OF SYRACUSE (406-367 B.C.)

Area controlled by Dionysius I

Taras Dependents and allies of Dionysius

Probable ally

Possible colonies in Adriatic (Ancona, Issa, Lissos), and alliance with Molossi

Victory over Lucanians 386

Dionysius married a Locrian

Destroyed by Dionysius (403)

Mercenaries settled

Heavily fortified. Visited by Plato 387

Attempt at their expulsion by Dionysius failed (398-7)

Taras

Heraclea

Metapontum

Thurii

LUCANIANS

Elea

R. Elleporus

Locri Epizephyrii

Naxos

Catana

Syracuse

Panormus

Solus

CARTHAGINIANS

R. Halycus

Motya

Carthage

0   50

Miles

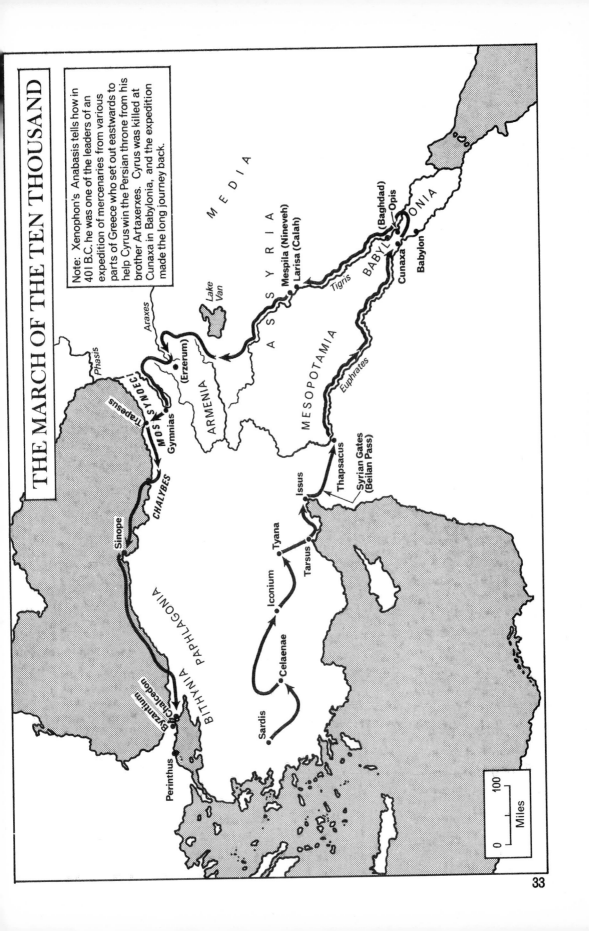

THE MARCH OF THE TEN THOUSAND

Note: Xenophon's *Anabasis* tells how in 401 B.C. he was one of the leaders of an expedition of mercenaries from various parts of Greece who set out eastwards to help Cyrus win the Persian throne from his brother Artaxerxes. Cyrus was killed at Cunaxa in Babylonia, and the expedition made the long journey back.

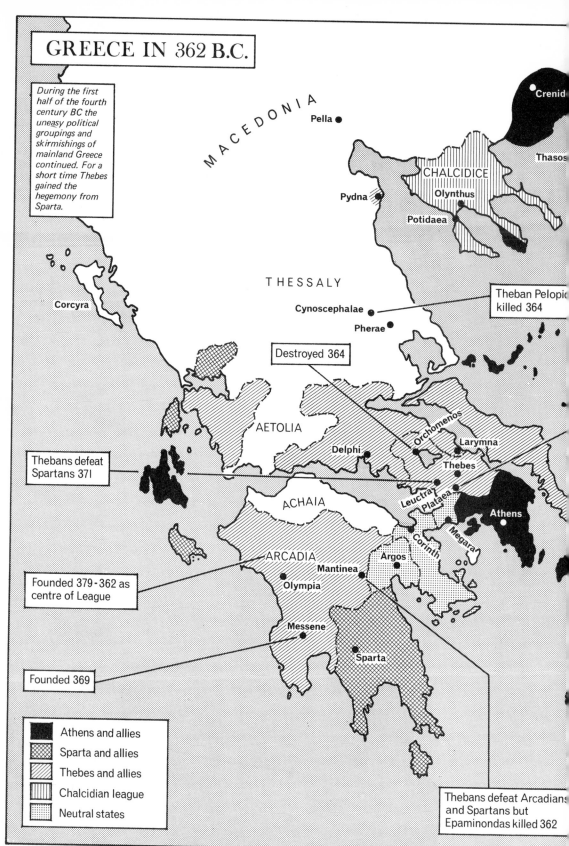

GREECE IN 362 B.C.

During the first half of the fourth century BC the uneasy political groupings and skirmishings of mainland Greece continued. For a short time Thebes gained the hegemony from Sparta.

MACEDONIA

Pella ●

Crenid

CHALCIDICE

Thasos

Olynthus ●

Pydna ●

Potidaea ●

THESSALY

Corcyra

Cynoscephalae ●

Theban Pelopid killed 364

Pherae ●

Destroyed 364

AETOLIA

Delphi ●

Orchomenos

Larymna ●

Thebans defeat Spartans 371

Thebes ●

Leuctra

Plataea

Athens ●

ACHAIA

Corinth

Megara

Founded 379-362 as centre of League

ARCADIA

Argos ●

Mantinea ●

Olympia ●

Messene ●

Sparta ●

Founded 369

■	Athens and allies
▨	Sparta and allies
▨	Thebes and allies
▥	Chalcidian league
▦	Neutral states

Thebans defeat Arcadians and Spartans but Epaminondas killed 362

34

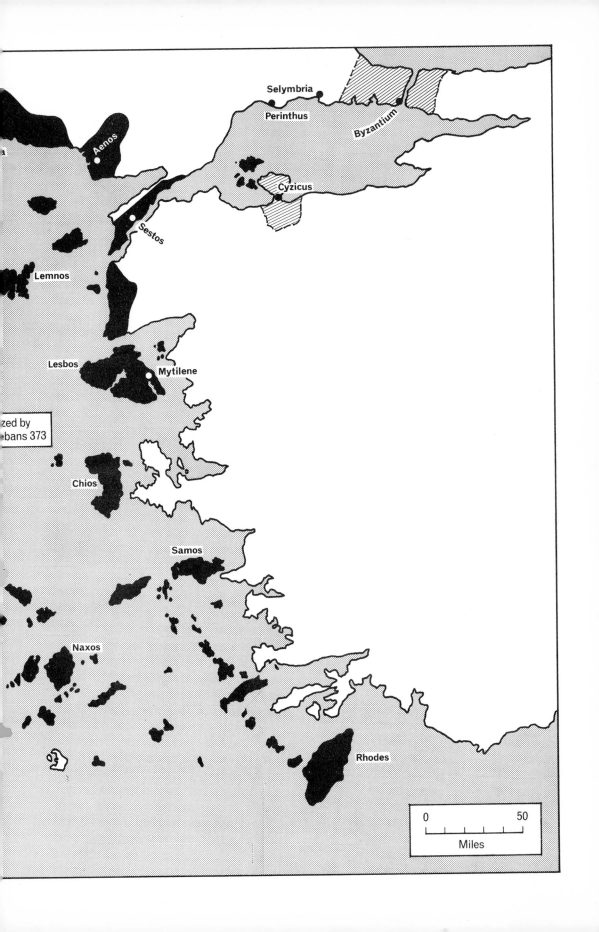

Selymbria

Perinthus

Byzantium

Aenos

Cyzicus

Sestos

Lemnos

Lesbos

Mytilene

zed by
·bans 373

Chios

Samos

Naxos

Rhodes

0   50

Miles

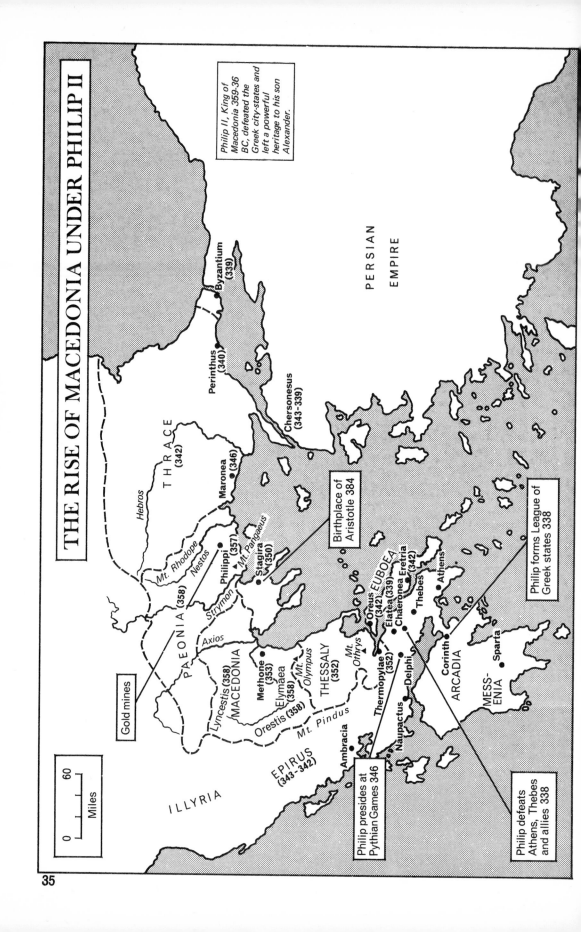

THE RISE OF MACEDONIA UNDER PHILIP II

Philip II, King of Macedonia 359-36 BC, defeated the Greek city-states and left a powerful heritage to his son Alexander.

PERSIAN EMPIRE

Byzantium (339)

Perinthus (340)

Chersonesus (343-339)

THRACE (342)

Maronea (346)

Hebros

Mt. Rhodope

Nestos

Mt. Pangaeus (350)

Philippi (357)

Stagira (350)

Birthplace of Aristotle 384

Strymon

PAEONIA (358)

Axios

Lyncestis (358)
MACEDONIA

Methone (353)

Elymaea (358)

Mt. Olympus

Orestis (358)

Mt. Pindus

THESSALY (352)

Mt. Othrys

EUBOEA

Oreus (342)

Elatea (339)

Chaeronea

Eretria (342)

Thebes

Athens

Thermopylae (352)

Delphi

Naupactus

Corinth

ARCADIA

MESS-
ENIA

Sparta

Philip forms League of Greek states 338

Gold mines

EPIRUS (343-342)

Ambracia

ILLYRIA

Philip presides at Pythian Games 346

Philip defeats Athens, Thebes and allies 338

0   60
Miles

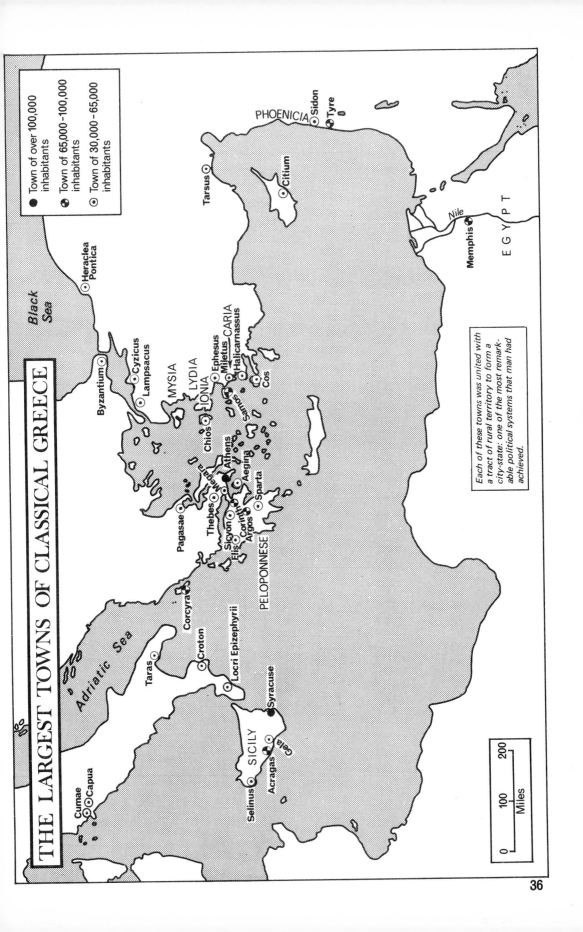

THE LARGEST TOWNS OF CLASSICAL GREECE

Town of over 100,000 inhabitants

Town of 65,000 - 100,000 inhabitants

Town of 30,000 - 65,000 inhabitants

Black Sea

Adriatic Sea

Cumae
Capua

Taras

Corcyra

Croton

Locri Epizephyrii

Syracuse

Gela

SICILY

Selinus

Acragas

Pagasae

Thebes

Sicyon

Elis

Corinth

Argos

PELOPONNESE

Megara

Athens

Aegina

Sparta

Chios

IONIA

LYDIA

MYSIA

Samos

Ephesus

Miletus CARIA

Halicarnassus

Cos

Byzantium

Lampsacus

Cyzicus

Heraclea Pontica

Tarsus

Citium

PHOENICIA

Sidon

Tyre

Nile

Memphis

E G Y P T

Each of these towns was united with a tract of rural territory to form a city-state: one of the most remarkable political systems that man had achieved.

0   100   200

Miles

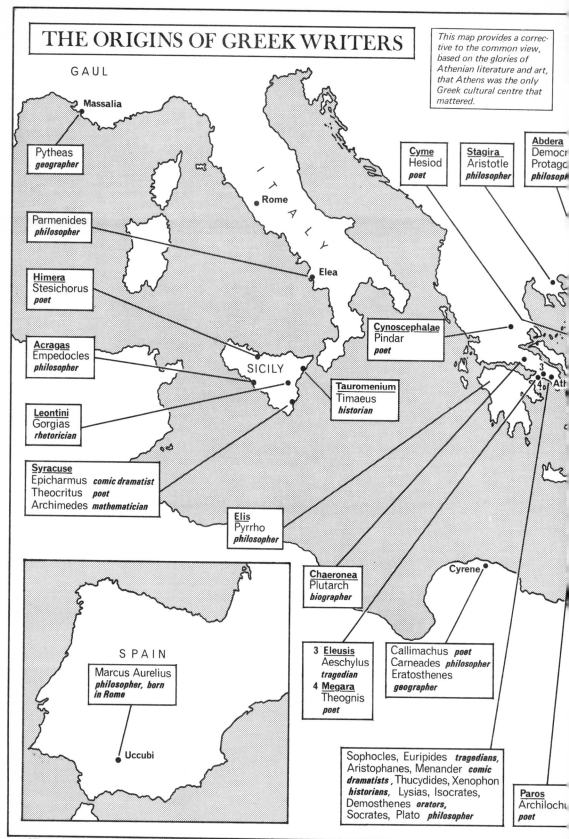

THE ORIGINS OF GREEK WRITERS

GAUL

This map provides a corrective to the common view, based on the glories of Athenian literature and art, that Athens was the only Greek cultural centre that mattered.

Massalia

Pytheas
geographer

Rome

I T A L Y

Parmenides
philosopher

Elea

Himera
Stesichorus
poet

Acragas
Empedocles
philosopher

SICILY

Leontini
Gorgias
rhetorician

Syracuse
Epicharmus   *comic dramatist*
Theocritus   *poet*
Archimedes   *mathematician*

Elis
Pyrrho
philosopher

Cyme
Hesiod
poet

Stagira
Aristotle
philosopher

Abdera
Democr
Protago
philosop

Cynoscephalae
Pindar
poet

Tauromenium
Timaeus
historian

Ath

Chaeronea
Plutarch
biographer

Cyrene

SPAIN

Marcus Aurelius
philosopher, born in Rome

Uccubi

3 Eleusis
Aeschylus
tragedian
4 Megara
Theognis
poet

Callimachus *poet*
Carneades *philosopher*
Eratosthenes
geographer

Sophocles, Euripides *tragedians*,
Aristophanes, Menander *comic dramatists*, Thucydides, Xenophon
historians, Lysias, Isocrates,
Demosthenes *orators*,
Socrates, Plato *philosopher*

Paros
Archiloch
poet

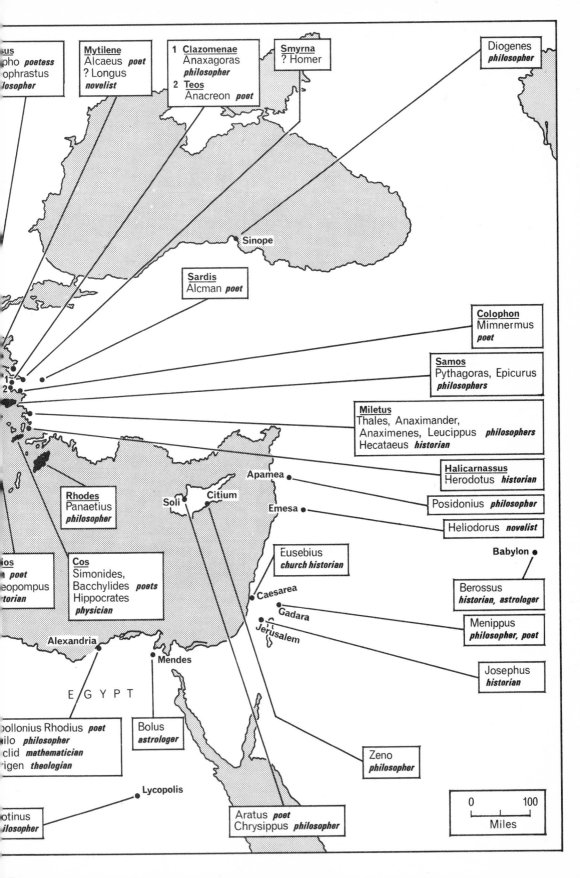

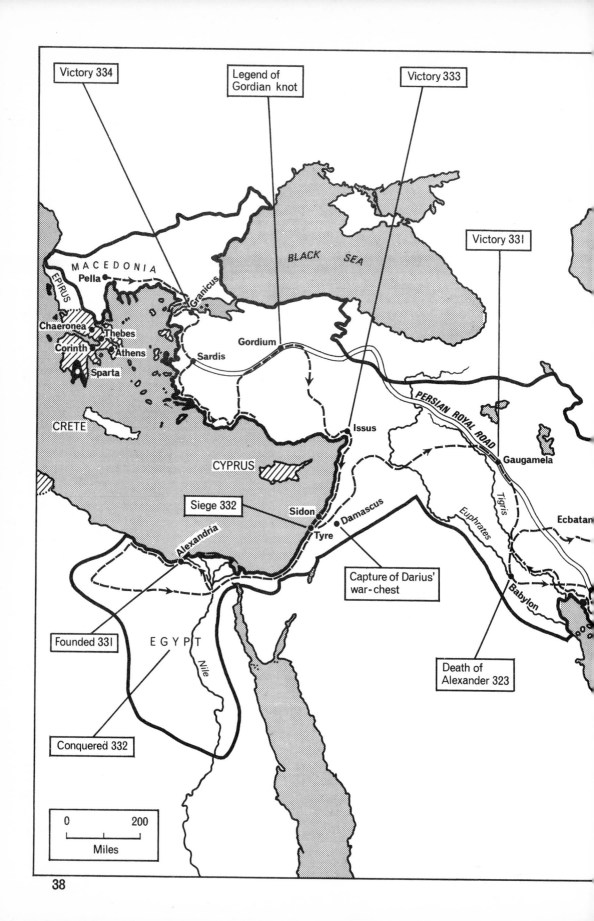

Victory 334

Legend of
Gordian knot

Victory 333

Victory 331

BLACK   SEA

MACEDONIA

EPIRUS

Pella

Granicus

Chaeronea

Thebes

Corinth

Athens

Sparta

Gordium

Sardis

PERSIAN ROYAL ROAD

CRETE

Issus

Gaugamela

CYPRUS

Siege 332

Sidon

Damascus

Tyre

Ecbatan

Tigris

Euphrates

Capture of Darius'
war-chest

Alexandria

Babylon

Founded 331

E G Y P T

Nile

Death of
Alexander 323

Conquered 332

0   200

Miles

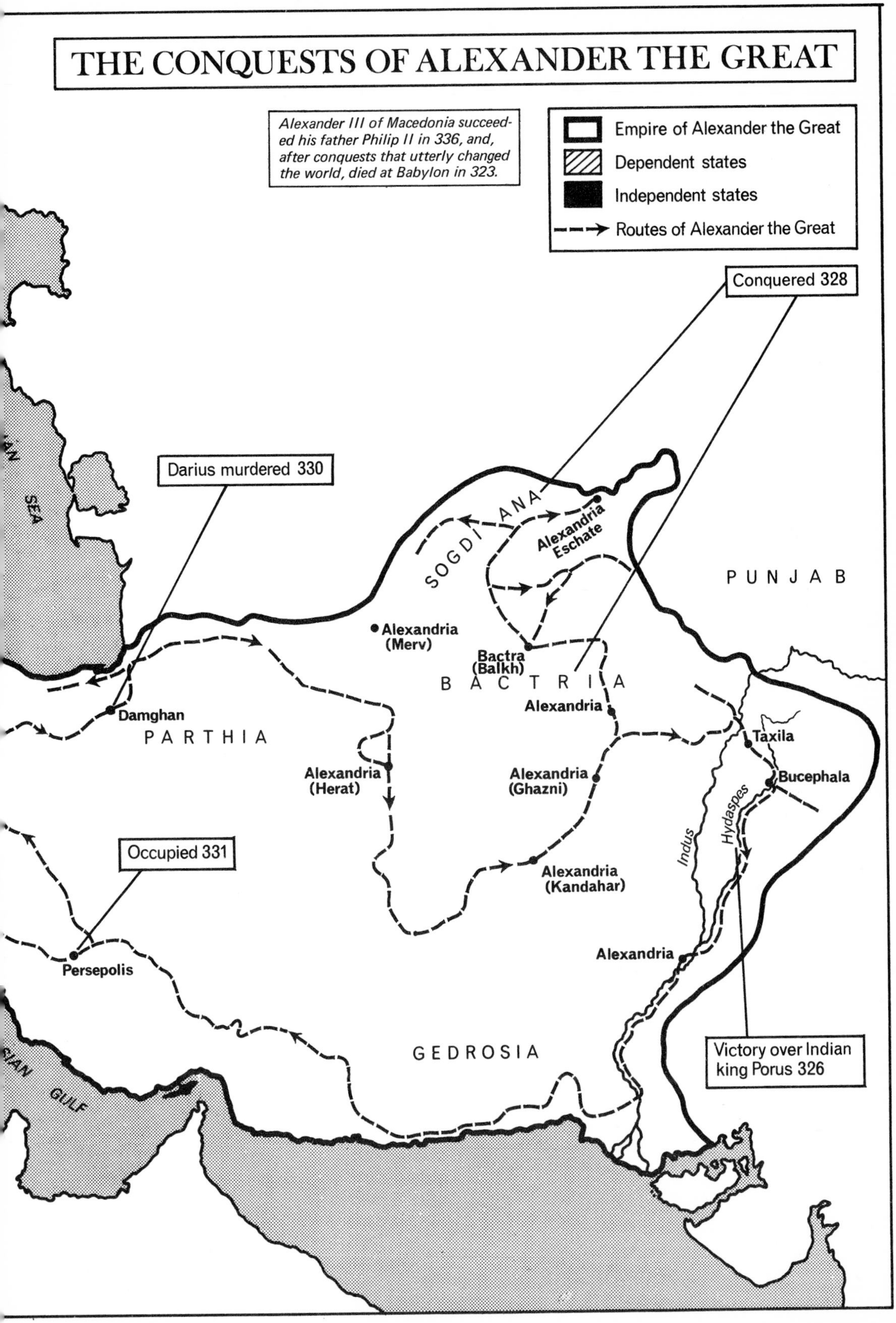

THE CONQUESTS OF ALEXANDER THE GREAT

Alexander III of Macedonia succeeded his father Philip II in 336, and, after conquests that utterly changed the world, died at Babylon in 323.

☐ Empire of Alexander the Great

▨ Dependent states

■ Independent states

- - ➤ Routes of Alexander the Great

Conquered 328

Darius murdered 330

PUNJAB

CASPIAN SEA

SOGDIANA

Alexandria Eschate

● Alexandria (Merv)

Bactra (Balkh)

BACTRIA

Alexandria

Taxila

● Damghan

PARTHIA

Alexandria (Herat)

Alexandria (Ghazni)

Bucephala

Indus

Hydaspes

Occupied 331

Alexandria (Kandahar)

Alexandria

● Persepolis

GEDROSIA

Victory over Indian king Porus 326

PERSIAN GULF

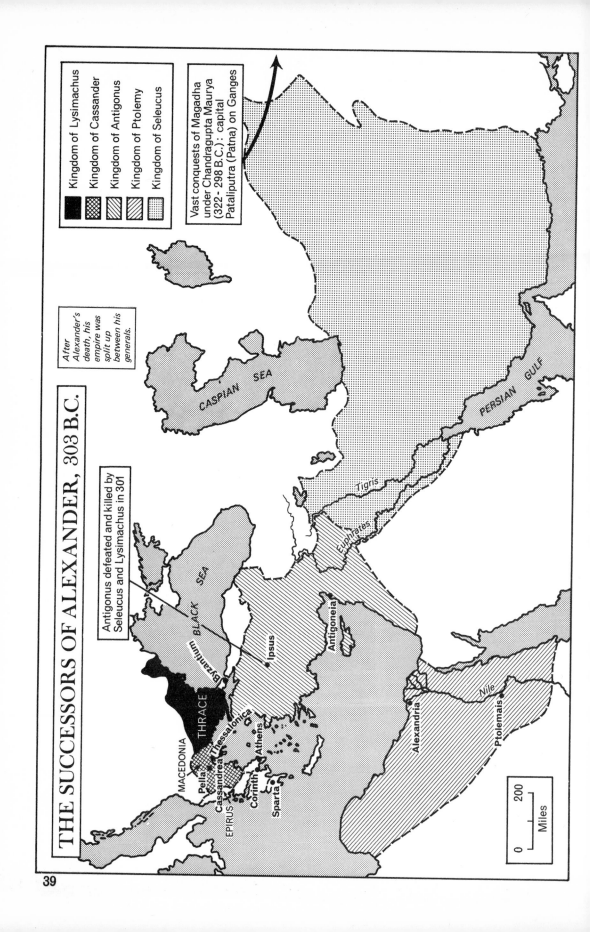

THE SUCCESSORS OF ALEXANDER, 303 B.C.

Kingdom of Lysimachus
Kingdom of Cassander
Kingdom of Antigonus
Kingdom of Ptolemy
Kingdom of Seleucus

Vast conquests of Magadha under Chandragupta Maurya (322 - 298 B.C.): capital Pataliputra (Patna) on Ganges

After Alexander's death, his empire was split up between his generals.

Antigonus defeated and killed by Seleucus and Lysimachus in 301

CASPIAN SEA

PERSIAN GULF

Tigris

Euphrates

BLACK SEA

Byzantium

THRACE

Ipsus

Antigoneia

Nile

MACEDONIA

Pella

Cassandrea

Thessalonica

Athens

Corinth

Sparta

EPIRUS

Alexandria

Ptolemais

0   200
Miles

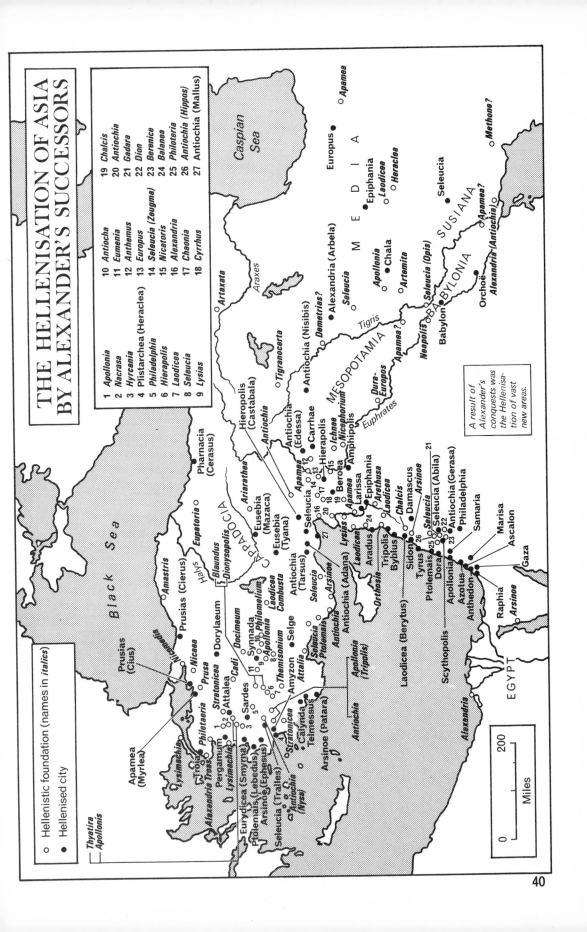

THE HELLENISATION OF ASIA BY ALEXANDER'S SUCCESSORS

○ Hellenistic foundation (names in *italics*)
● Hellenised city

Thyatira
Apollonis

1 *Apollonia*
2 *Nacrasa*
3 *Hyrcania*
4 *Plistarchea (Heraclea)*
5 *Philadelphia*
6 *Hierapolis*
7 *Laodicea*
8 *Seleucia*
9 *Lysias*

10 *Antiocha*
11 *Eumenia*
12 *Anthemus*
13 *Europus*
14 *Seleucia (Zeugma)*
15 *Nicatoris*
16 *Alexandria*
17 *Chaonia*
18 *Cyrrhus*

19 *Chalcis*
20 *Antiochia*
21 *Gadara*
22 *Dion*
23 *Berenice*
24 *Balanea*
25 *Philoteria*
26 *Antiochia (Hippos)*
27 Antiochia (Mallus)

A result of Alexander's conquests was the Hellenisation of vast new areas.

40

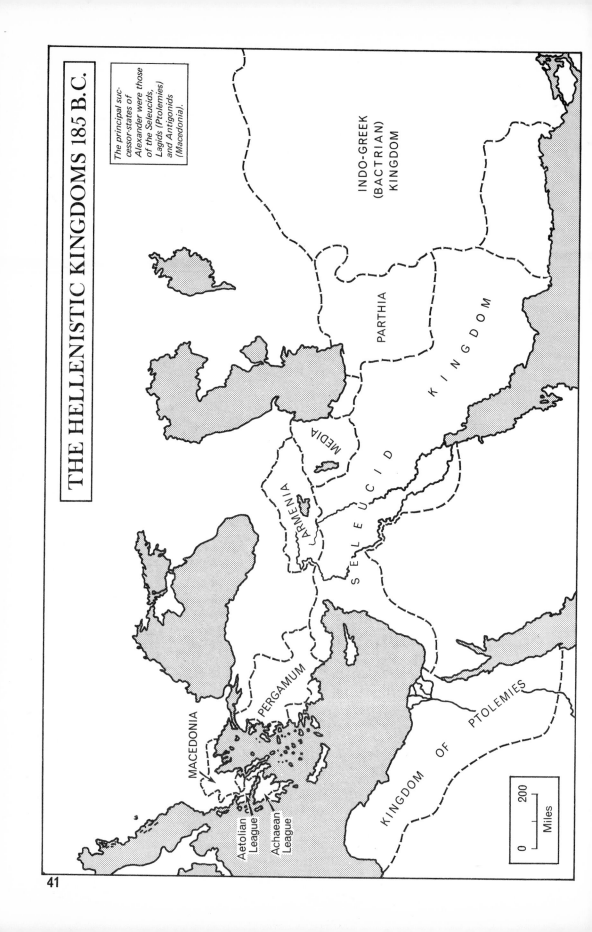

THE HELLENISTIC KINGDOMS 185 B.C.

The principal suc-
cessor-states of
Alexander were those
of the Seleucids,
Lagids (Ptolemies)
and Antigonids
(Macedonia).

INDO-GREEK
(BACTRIAN)
KINGDOM

PARTHIA

MEDIA

ARMENIA

SELEUCID

KINGDOM

PERGAMUM

MACEDONIA

Aetolian
League

Achaean
League

KINGDOM OF PTOLEMIES

0   200
Miles

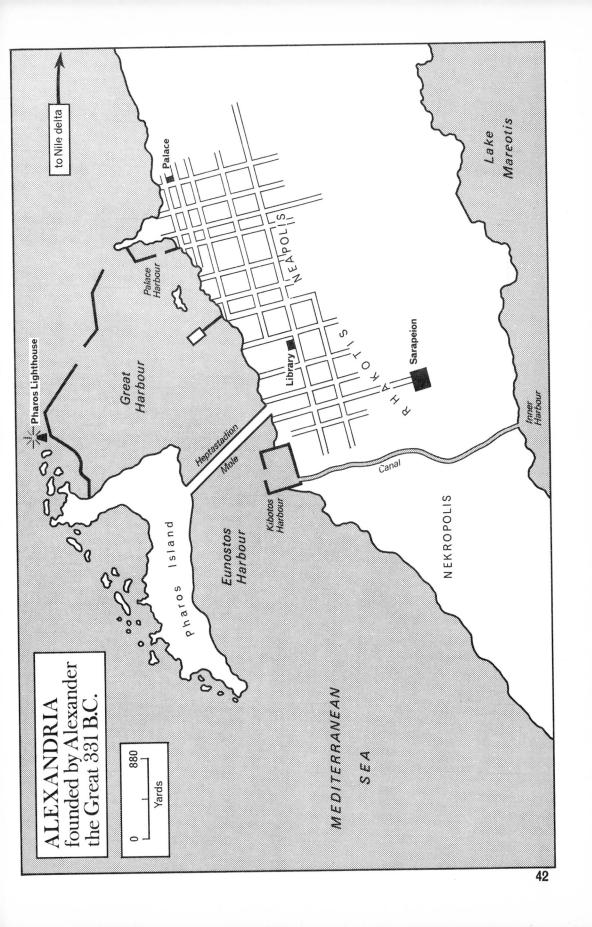

ALEXANDRIA
founded by Alexander
the Great 331 B.C.

0   880
Yards

to Nile delta

MEDITERRANEAN SEA

Pharos Island

Pharos Lighthouse

Great Harbour

Palace Harbour

Palace

NEAPOLIS

Library

RHAKOTIS

Sarapeion

Heptastadion Mole

Eunostos Harbour

Kibotos Harbour

Canal

NEKROPOLIS

Inner Harbour

Lake Mareotis

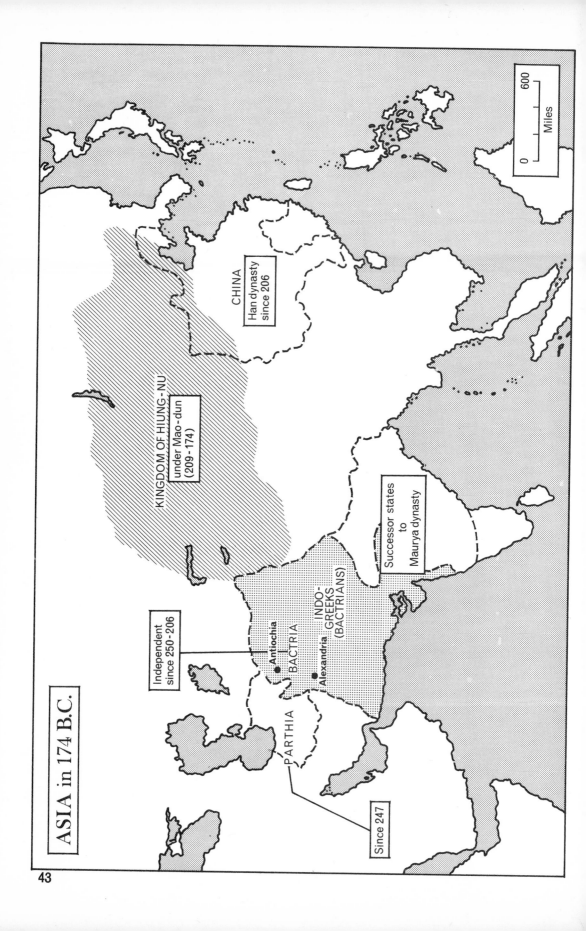

ASIA in 174 B.C.

KINGDOM OF HIUNG-NU
under Mao-dun
(209-174)

CHINA
Han dynasty
since 206

Successor states
to
Maurya dynasty

INDO-
GREEKS
(BACTRIANS)

Independent
since 250-206

Antiochia
BACTRIA

Alexandria

PARTHIA

Since 247

600

Miles

0

43

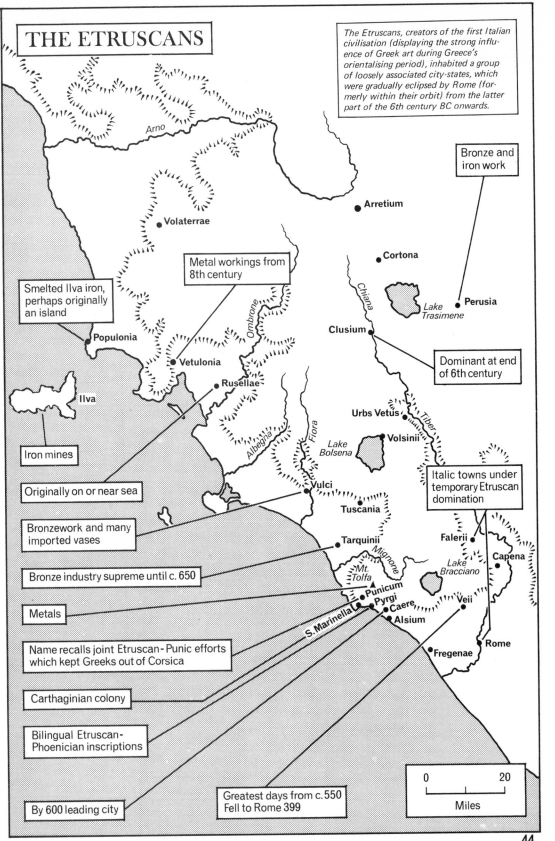

THE ETRUSCANS

The Etruscans, creators of the first Italian civilisation (displaying the strong influence of Greek art during Greece's orientalising period), inhabited a group of loosely associated city-states, which were gradually eclipsed by Rome (formerly within their orbit) from the latter part of the 6th century BC onwards.

Arno

Bronze and iron work

• **Arretium**

• **Volaterrae**

• **Cortona**

Metal workings from 8th century

Chiana

Smelted Ilva iron, perhaps originally an island

Ombrone

Perusia

Lake Trasimene

Clusium

Populonia

• **Vetulonia**

Dominant at end of 6th century

• **Rusellae**

Ilva

Urbs Vetus

Tiber

Iron mines

Fiora

Lake Bolsena

Volsinii

Albegna

Originally on or near sea

Italic towns under temporary Etruscan domination

Bronzework and many imported vases

Vulci

Tuscania

Bronze industry supreme until c. 650

Falerii

Tarquinii

Mignone

Capena

Lake Bracciano

Metals

Mt. Tolfa

Punicum

Pyrgi

Veii

Name recalls joint Etruscan-Punic efforts which kept Greeks out of Corsica

S. Marinella

Caere

Alsium

Rome

Carthaginian colony

Fregenae

Bilingual Etruscan-Phoenician inscriptions

By 600 leading city

Greatest days from c.550 Fell to Rome 399

0   20

Miles

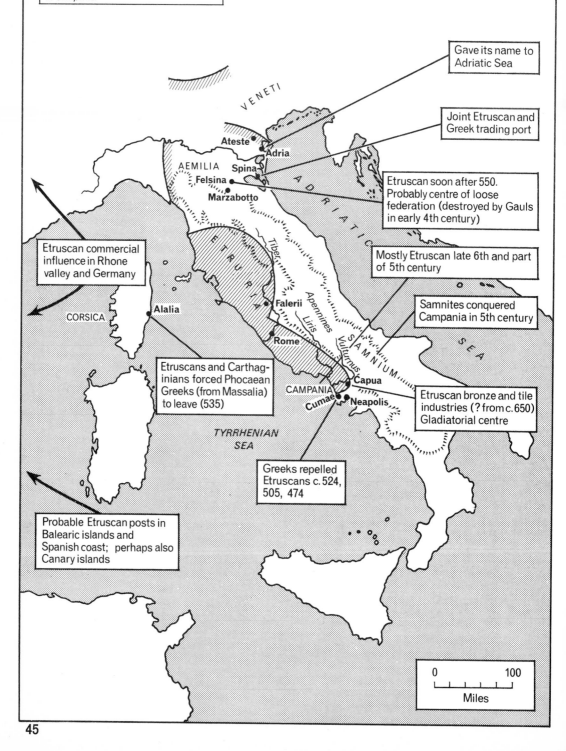

ETRUSCAN EXPANSION

At the height of their power the Etruscans possessed two empires, one north of the Apennines and the other to the South-east, in Campania.

Gave its name to Adriatic Sea

Joint Etruscan and Greek trading port

Etruscan soon after 550. Probably centre of loose federation (destroyed by Gauls in early 4th century)

Mostly Etruscan late 6th and part of 5th century

Etruscan commercial influence in Rhone valley and Germany

Samnites conquered Campania in 5th century

Etruscans and Carthaginians forced Phocaean Greeks (from Massalia) to leave (535)

Etruscan bronze and tile industries (? from c.650) Gladiatorial centre

Greeks repelled Etruscans c.524, 505, 474

Probable Etruscan posts in Balearic islands and Spanish coast; perhaps also Canary islands

VENETI

Ateste
Adria
AEMILIA Spina
Felsina
Marzabotto

ADRIATIC

ETRURIA
Tiber
Falerii
Apennines
Liris
Rome
Vulturnus
SAMNIUM

CORSICA
Alalia

CAMPANIA
Capua
Cumae Neapolis

SEA

TYRRHENIAN
SEA

0   100
Miles

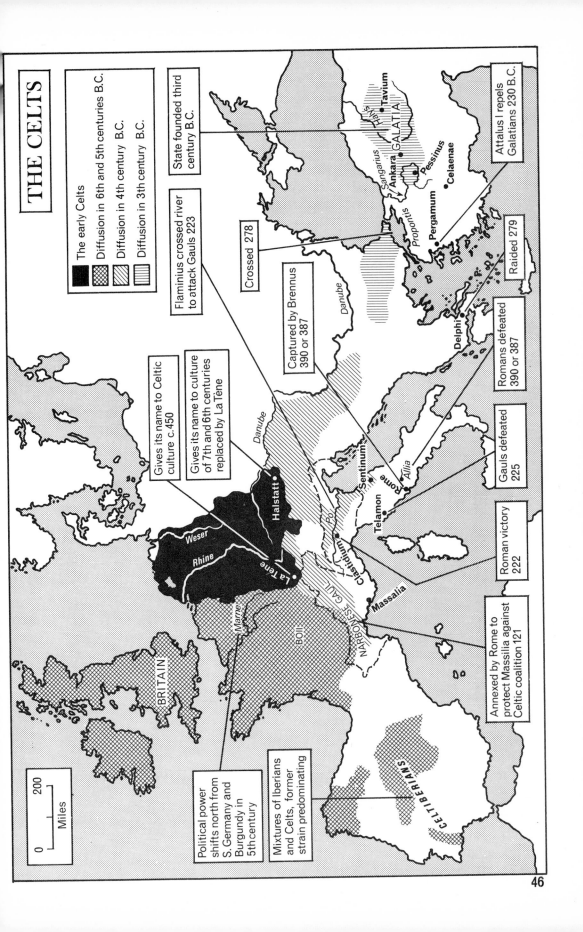

THE CELTS

Legend:
- The early Celts
- Diffusion in 6th and 5th centuries B.C.
- Diffusion in 4th century B.C.
- Diffusion in 3th century B.C.

State founded third century B.C.

Flaminius crossed river to attack Gauls 223

Crossed 278

Captured by Brennus 390 or 387

Gives its name to Celtic culture c.450

Gives its name to culture of 7th and 6th centuries replaced by La Tène

Political power shifts north from S. Germany and Burgundy in 5th century

Mixtures of Iberians and Celts, former strain predominating

Attalus I repels Galatians 230 B.C.

Raided 279

Romans defeated 390 or 387

Gauls defeated 225

Roman victory 222

Annexed by Rome to protect Massilia against Celtic coalition 121

Place labels:
Ister, Tavium, GALATIA, Ankara, Sangarius, Pessinus, Celaenae, Propontis, Pergamum, Delphi, Danube, Danube, Halstatt, Weser, Rhine, La Tène, Marne, BRITAIN, BOII, Po, Clastidium, GAUL, NARBONESE GAUL, Sentinum, Rome, Allia, Telamon, Massalia, CELTIBERIANS

0 200 Miles

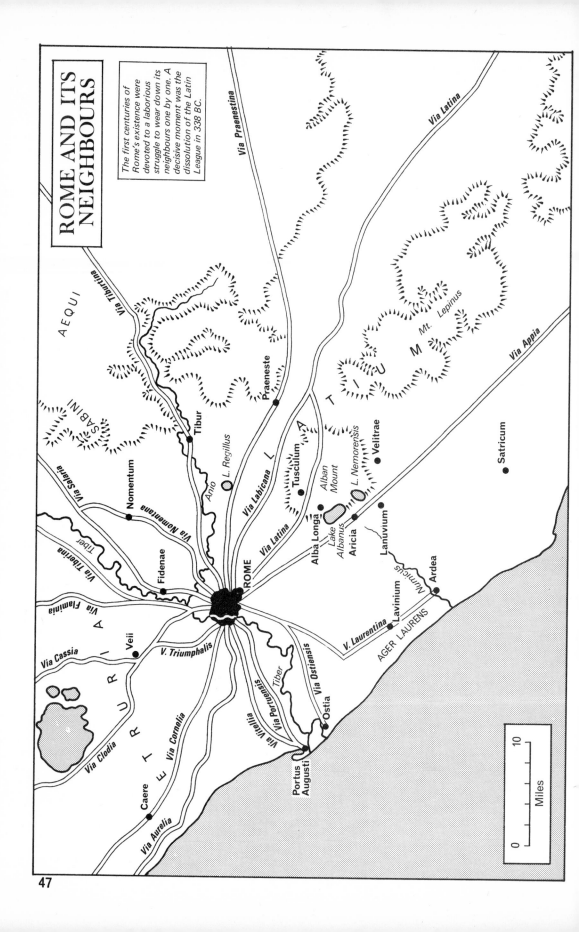

ROME AND ITS NEIGHBOURS

The first centuries of Rome's existence were devoted to a laborious struggle to wear down its neighbours one by one. A decisive moment was the dissolution of the Latin League in 338 BC.

47

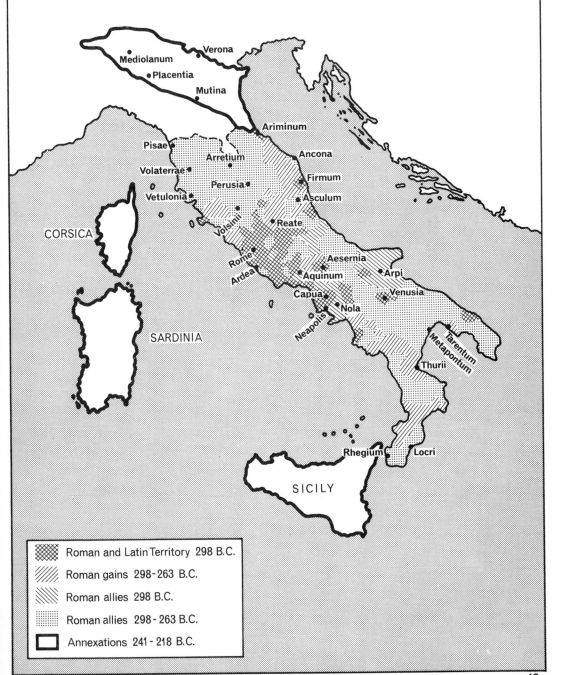

ROME'S CONQUEST OF ITALY

Third Samnite War 298-290
Invasion of Pyrrhus 280-275
First Punic War 264-241
Second Punic War 218-201
(see separate map)

Verona

Mediolanum

Placentia

Mutina

Ariminum

Pisae

Arretium

Ancona

Volaterrae

Firmum

Perusia

Asculum

Vetulonia

Volsinii

Reate

CORSICA

Rome

Aesernia

Ardea

Aquinum

Arpi

Capua

Venusia

Nola

SARDINIA

Neapolis

Tarentum

Metapontum

Thurii

Rhegium

Locri

SICILY

▨ Roman and Latin Territory 298 B.C.
▨ Roman gains 298-263 B.C.
▨ Roman allies 298 B.C.
▨ Roman allies 298-263 B.C.
▢ Annexations 241-218 B.C.

THE ROADS OF ROMAN ITALY

0   100
Miles

Augusta Praetoria
Mediolanum
Segusio
Dertona
Genua
Luna
Pisae
Vada Volaterrana
Placentia
Cremona
Verona
Mantua
Ravenna
Ariminum
Florentia
Fanum Fortunae
Arretium
Truentum
Aternum
Reate
Tibur
Corfinium
ROME
Anagnia
Fregellae
Tarracina
Cales
Casilinum
Neapolis
Capua
Beneventum
Canusium
Venusia
Brundisium
Tarentum
Rhegium
Aquileia

CORSICA

SARDINIA

TYRRHENIAN SEA

ADRIATIC SEA

SICILY

1 Via Aemilia (187 B.C.)	**8** Via Julia Augusta
2 Via Appia (312-244 B.C.)	**9** Via Domitiana
3 Via Aurelia	**10** Via Trajana
4 Via Flaminia (220 B.C.)	**11** Via Cassia
5 Via Latina	**12** Via Popillia
6 Via Postumia (148 B.C.)	**13** Via Salaria
7 Via Valeria	

THE WESTERN MEDITERRANEAN IN 270 B.C.

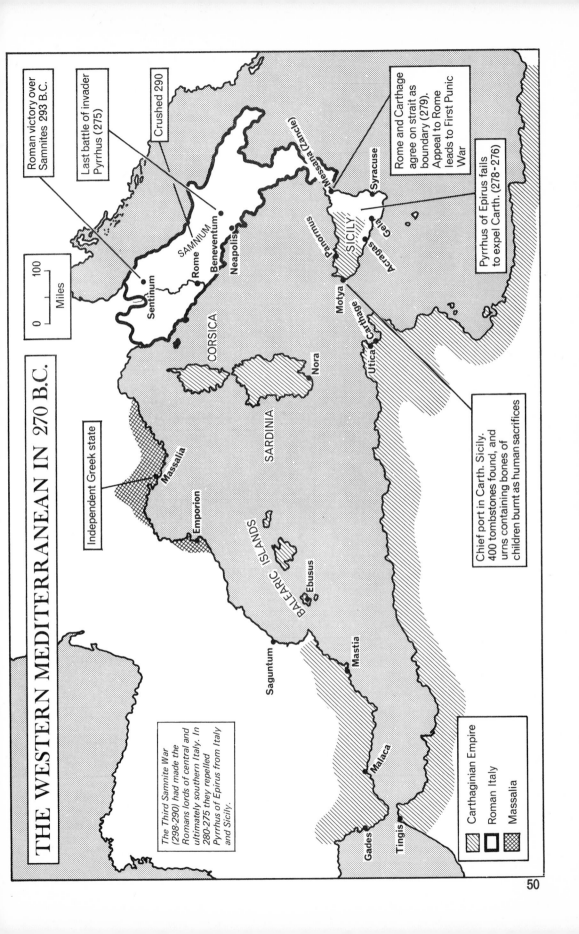

Roman victory over Samnites 293 B.C.

Last battle of invader Pyrrhus (275)

Crushed 290

Rome and Carthage agree on strait as boundary (279). Appeal to Rome leads to First Punic War

Pyrrhus of Epirus fails to expel Carth. (278-276)

Chief port in Carth. Sicily. 400 tombstones found, and urns containing bones of children burnt as human sacrifices

Independent Greek state

The Third Samnite War (298-290) had made the Romans lords of central and ultimately southern Italy. In 280-275 they repelled Pyrrhus of Epirus from Italy and Sicily.

0   100
Miles

SAMNIUM

Rome

Sentinum

Beneventum

Neapolis

Messana (Zancle)

Panormus

Syracuse

SICILY

Acragas

Gela

Motya

Carthage

Utica

CORSICA

Nora

SARDINIA

Massalia

Emporion

BALEARIC ISLANDS

Ebusus

Saguntum

Mastia

Malaca

Gades

Tingis

Carthaginian Empire

Roman Italy

Massalia

50

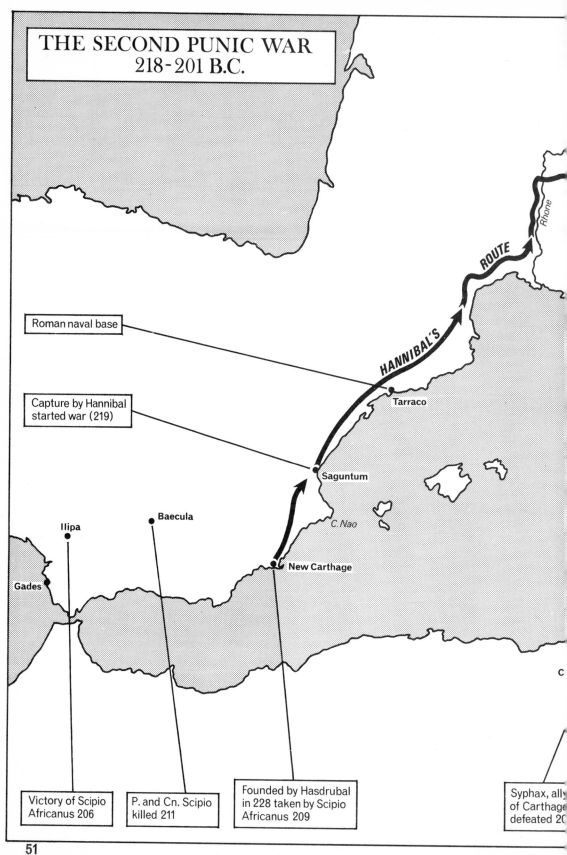

THE SECOND PUNIC WAR
218-201 B.C.

Roman naval base

Capture by Hannibal started war (219)

HANNIBAL'S ROUTE

Rhone

Tarraco

Saguntum

C. Nao

Ilipa

Baecula

New Carthage

Gades

Victory of Scipio Africanus 206

P. and Cn. Scipio killed 211

Founded by Hasdrubal in 228 taken by Scipio Africanus 209

Syphax, ally of Carthage defeated 20

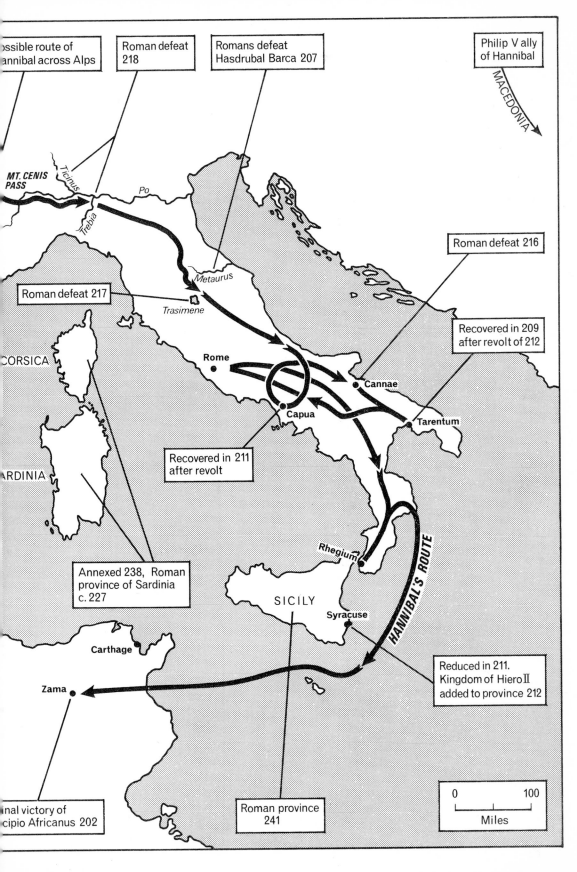

ossible route of
annibal across Alps

Roman defeat
218

Romans defeat
Hasdrubal Barca 207

Philip V ally
of Hannibal

MACEDONIA

MT. CENIS
PASS

Ticinus

Po

Trebia

Metaurus

Roman defeat 217

Trasimene

Roman defeat 216

CORSICA

Rome

Cannae

Recovered in 209
after revolt of 212

Capua

Tarentum

Recovered in 211
after revolt

ARDINIA

Annexed 238, Roman
province of Sardinia
c. 227

Rhegium

HANNIBAL'S ROUTE

SICILY

Syracuse

Carthage

Reduced in 211.
Kingdom of Hiero II
added to province 212

Zama

inal victory of
cipio Africanus 202

Roman province
241

0   100

Miles

E

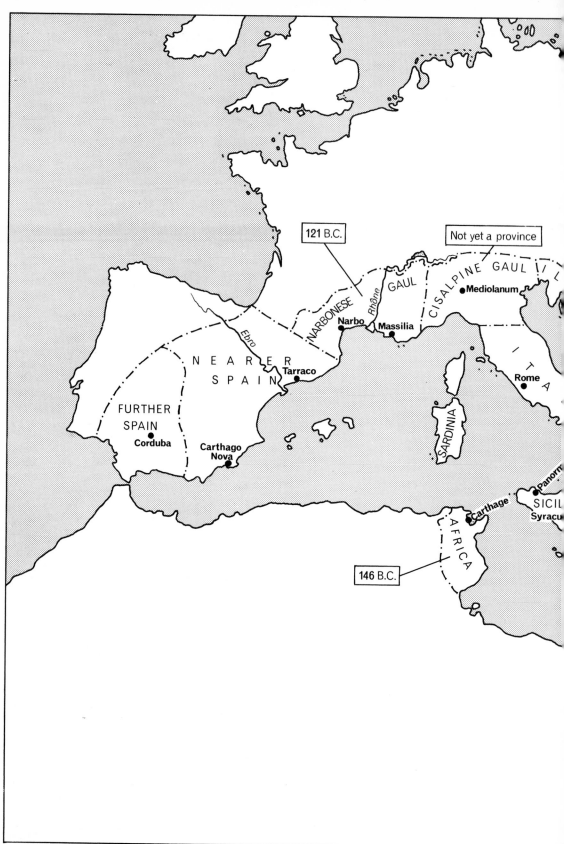

121 B.C.

Not yet a province

GAUL

CISALPINE GAUL

Mediolanum

NARBONESE

Rhône

Narbo

Massilia

Rome

N E A R E R
S P A I N

Ebro

Tarraco

SARDINIA

FURTHER
SPAIN

Corduba

Carthago
Nova

Panorm

SICIL

Carthage

Syracu

AFRICA

146 B.C.

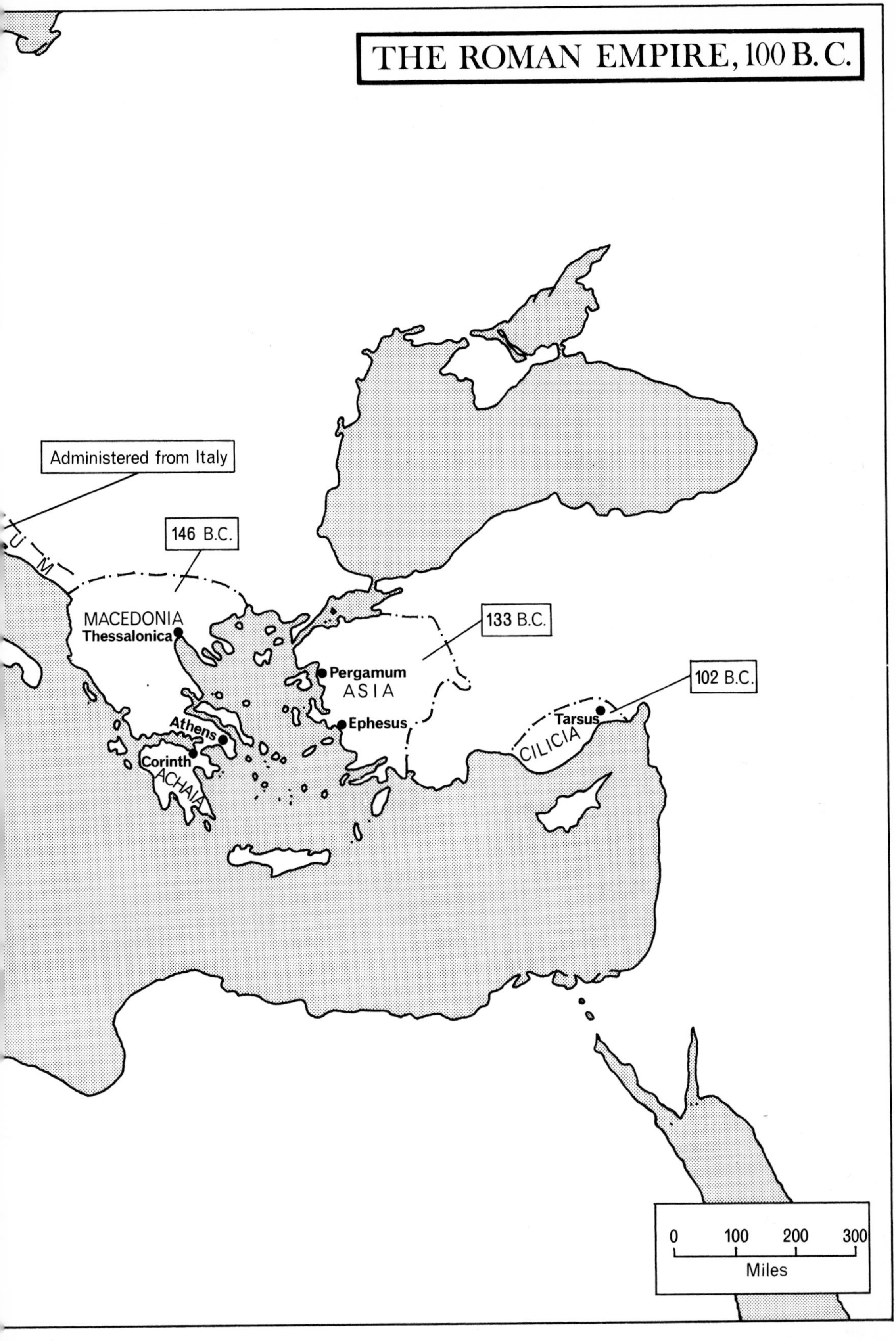

THE ROMAN EMPIRE, 100 B.C.

Administered from Italy

146 B.C.

133 B.C.

102 B.C.

MACEDONIA
Thessalonica

Pergamum
ASIA

Athens

Ephesus

Corinth
ACHAIA

Tarsus
CILICIA

0	100	200	300

Miles

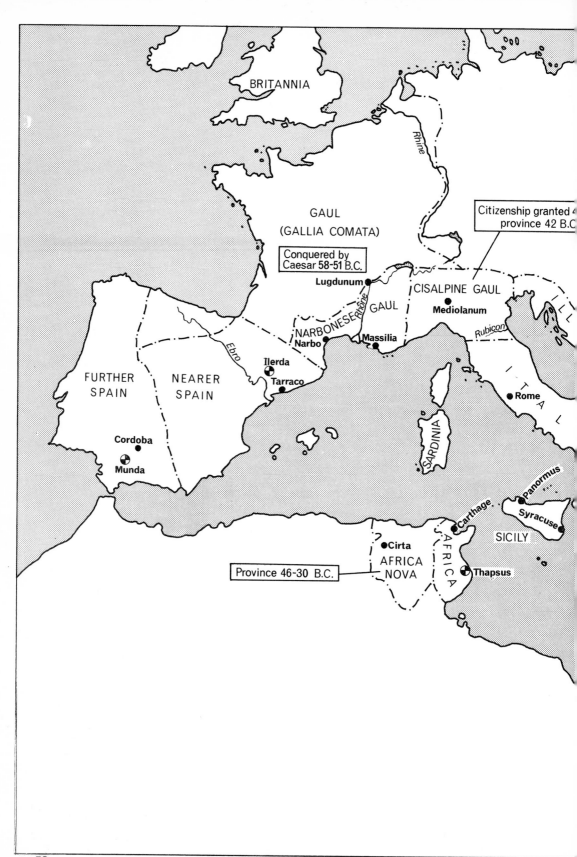

BRITANNIA

Rhine

GAUL
(GALLIA COMATA)

Citizenship granted
province 42 B.C

Conquered by
Caesar 58-51 B.C.

Lugdunum

CISALPINE GAUL

Mediolanum

Rhône

GAUL

NARBONESE
Narbo

Massilia

Rubicon

Ebro

Ilerda

Tarraco

FURTHER
SPAIN

NEARER
SPAIN

Rome

SARDINIA

ITALY

Cordoba

Munda

Panormus

Carthage

Syracuse

SICILY

Cirta

AFRICA
NOVA

AFRICA

Province 46-30 B.C.

Thapsus

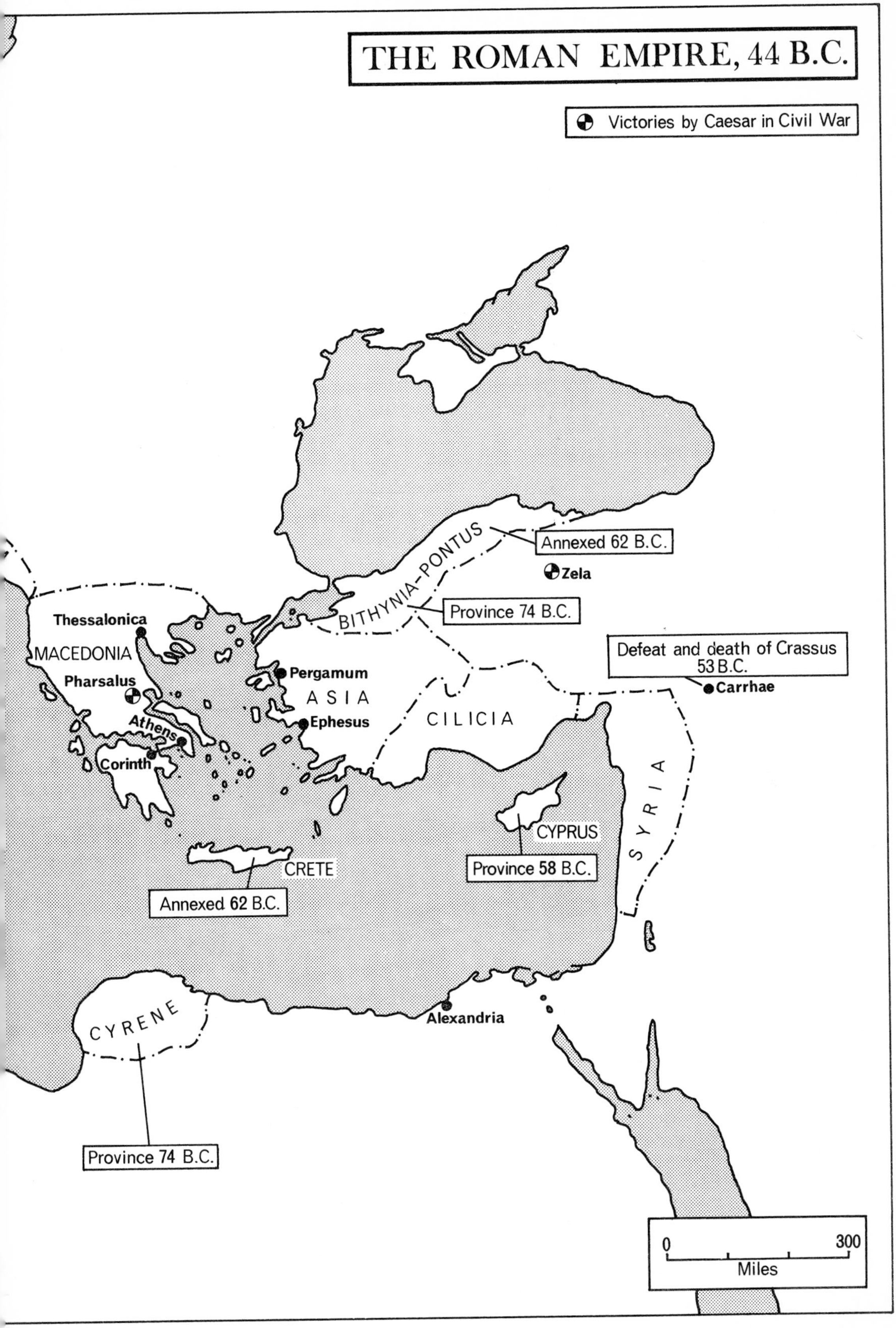

THE ROMAN EMPIRE, 44 B.C.

Annexed 62 B.C.

⊕ **Zela**

Province 74 B.C.

BITHYNIA-PONTUS

Defeat and death of Crassus
53 B.C.

● **Carrhae**

Thessalonica

MACEDONIA

Pharsalus ⊕

A S I A

Pergamum ●

Athens ●

Ephesus ●

C I L I C I A

Corinth ●

S Y R I A

CYPRUS

CRETE

Province 58 B.C.

Annexed 62 B.C.

C Y R E N E

Alexandria ●

Province 74 B.C.

0 ————————— 300

Miles

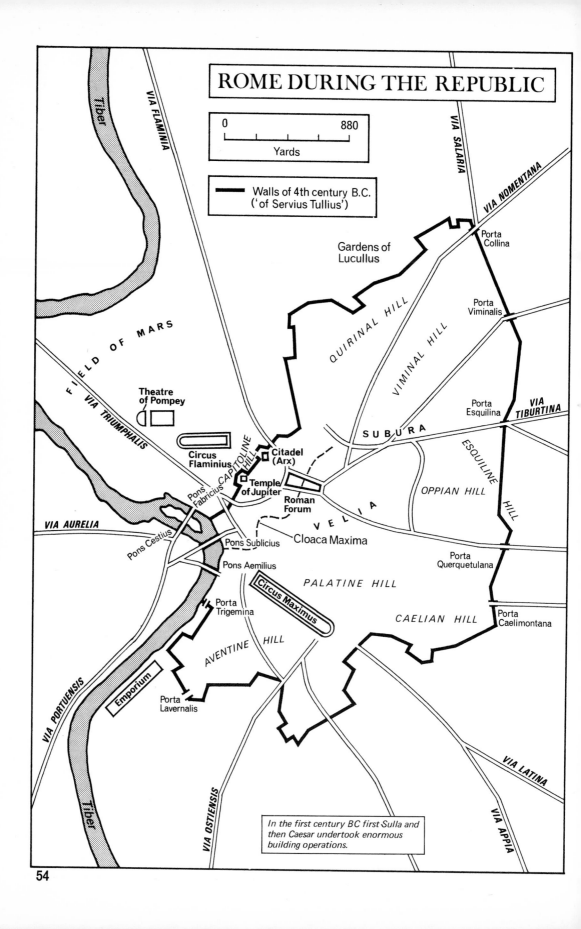

ROME DURING THE REPUBLIC

0   880

Yards

━━━━ Walls of 4th century B.C.
('of Servius Tullius')

Tiber

VIA FLAMINIA

VIA SALARIA

VIA NOMENTANA

Porta
Collina

Gardens of
Lucullus

Porta
Viminalis

QUIRINAL HILL

VIMINAL HILL

FIELD OF MARS

VIA TRIUMPHALIS

Porta
Esquilina

VIA
TIBURTINA

Theatre
of Pompey

SUBURA

ESQUILINE
HILL

Circus
Flaminius

CAPITOLINE HILL

Citadel
(Arx)

OPPIAN HILL

Pons
Fabricius

Temple
of Jupiter

Roman
Forum

VIA AURELIA

VELIA

Pons Cestius

Cloaca Maxima

Pons Sublicius

Porta
Querquetulana

Pons Aemilius

PALATINE HILL

Porta
Trigemina

Circus Maximus

CAELIAN HILL

Porta
Caelimontana

AVENTINE HILL

VIA PORTUENSIS

Emporium

Porta
Lavernalis

VIA OSTIENSIS

VIA LATINA

VIA APPIA

Tiber

In the first century BC first Sulla and
then Caesar undertook enormous
building operations.

54

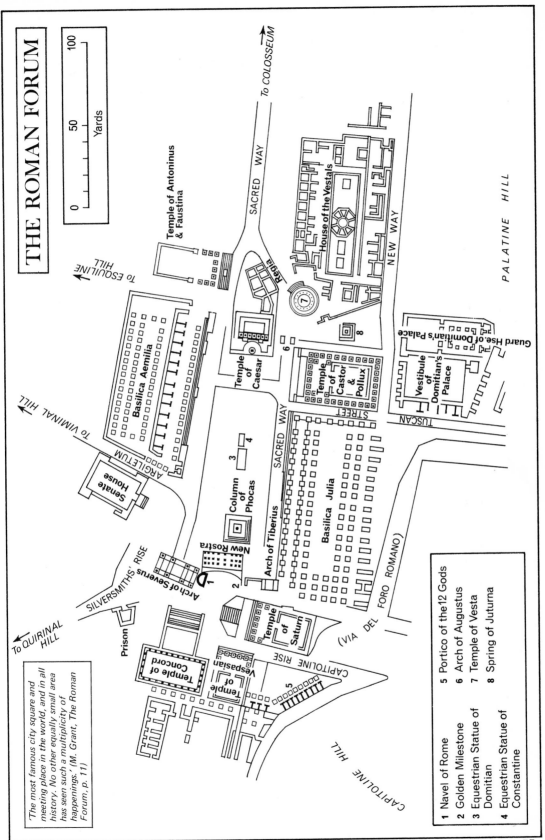

THE ROMAN FORUM

Yards

0   50   100

'The most famous city square and meeting place in the world, and in all history. No other equally small area has seen such a multiplicity of happenings.' (M. Grant, The Roman Forum, p. 11)

To ESQUILINE HILL

Temple of Antoninus & Faustina

SACRED WAY

To COLOSSEUM

Regia

House of the Vestals

NEW WAY

PALATINE HILL

To VIMINAL HILL

Basilica Aemilia

ARGILETUM

Senate House

Temple of Caesar

7

8

Temple of Castor & Pollux

6

Guard Hse. of Domitian's Palace

Vestibule of Domitian's Palace

TUSCAN   STREET

Column of Phocas

3

4

Arch of Tiberius

SACRED WAY

Basilica Julia

SILVERSMITHS' RISE

New Rostra

Arch of Severus

1

2

(VIA DEL FORO ROMANO)

To QUIRINAL HILL

Prison

Temple of Concord

Temple of Vespasian

Temple of Saturn

5

CAPITOLINE RISE

CAPITOLINE HILL

1 Navel of Rome
2 Golden Milestone
3 Equestrian Statue of Domitian
4 Equestrian Statue of Constantine

5 Portico of the12 Gods
6 Arch of Augustus
7 Temple of Vesta
8 Spring of Juturna

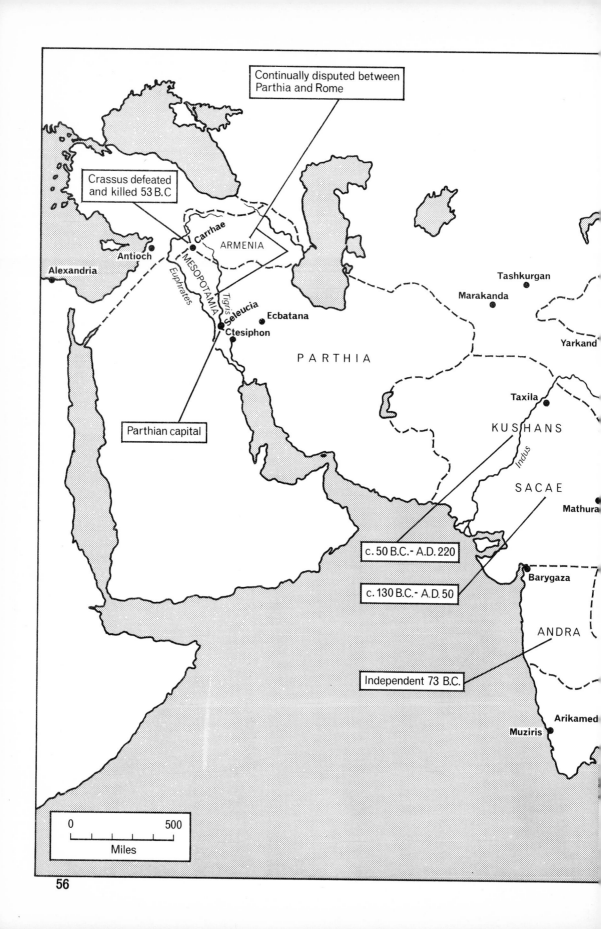

Continually disputed between
Parthia and Rome

Crassus defeated
and killed 53 B.C

Carrhae

ARMENIA

Antioch

Alexandria

MESOPOTAMIA

Euphrates

Tigris

Seleucia

Ecbatana

Ctesiphon

PARTHIA

Tashkurgan

Marakanda

Yarkand

Parthian capital

Taxila

KUSHANS

Indus

SACAE

Mathura

c. 50 B.C.- A.D. 220

c. 130 B.C.- A.D. 50

Barygaza

ANDRA

Independent 73 B.C.

Arikamed

Muziris

0   500

Miles

PARTHIA AND THE EAST

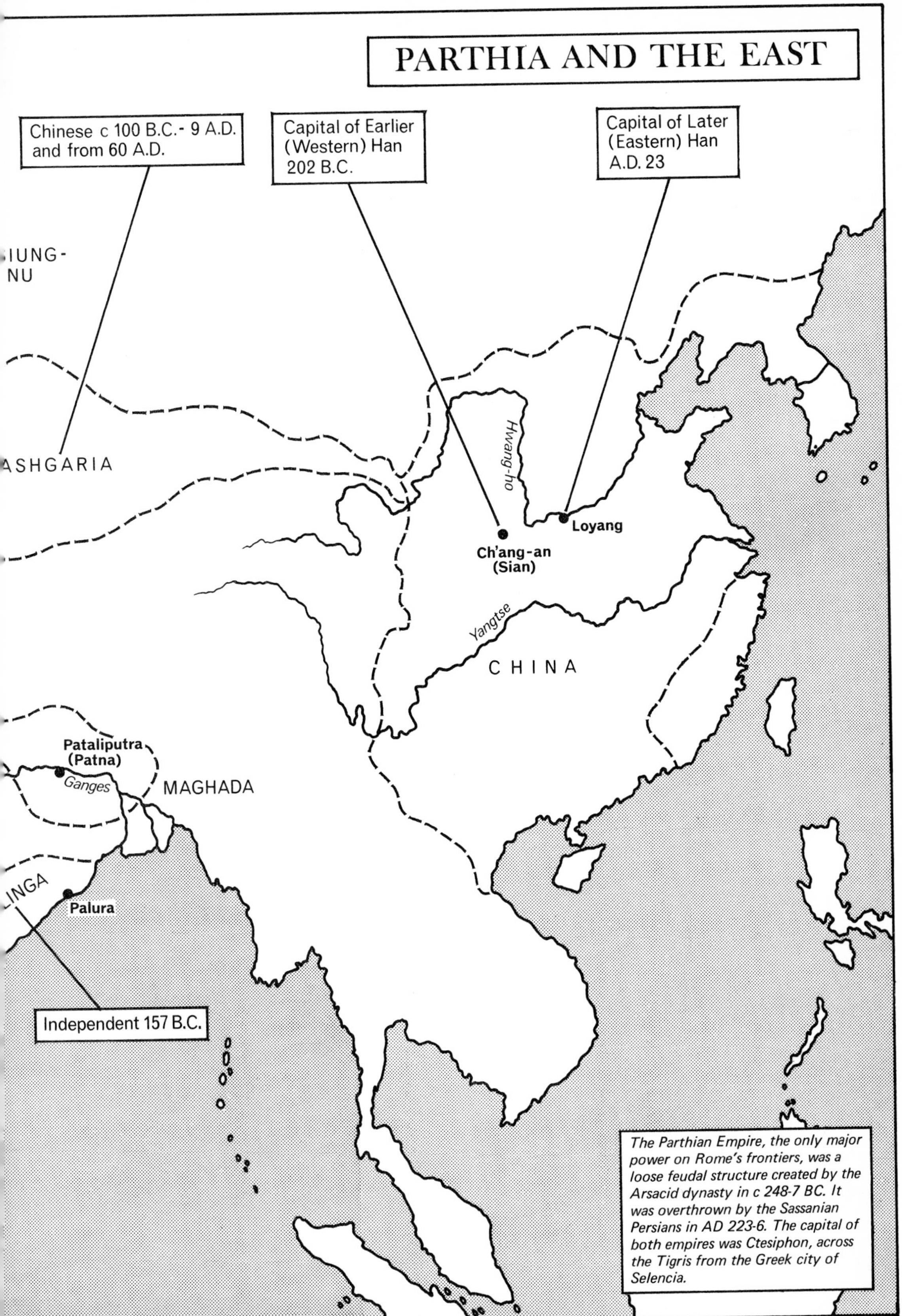

Chinese c 100 B.C.- 9 A.D. and from 60 A.D.

Capital of Earlier (Western) Han 202 B.C.

Capital of Later (Eastern) Han A.D. 23

IUNG-NU

ASHGARIA

Hwang-ho

Loyang

Ch'ang-an (Sian)

Yangtse

CHINA

Pataliputra (Patna)

Ganges

MAGHADA

LINGA

Palura

Independent 157 B.C.

The Parthian Empire, the only major power on Rome's frontiers, was a loose feudal structure created by the Arsacid dynasty in c 248-7 BC. It was overthrown by the Sassanian Persians in AD 223-6. The capital of both empires was Ctesiphon, across the Tigris from the Greek city of Selencia.

BRITANNIA

FREE GERMANY

LWR. GERMANY (17 B.C.)

Temporarily conquered from 15 B.C. but abandoned after ambushing of Varus by Arminius in A.D. 9

Colonia Agrippinensis

Rhine

BELGICA

Moguntiacum

LOWER PANNONIA (10 B.)

LUGDUNENSIS

UPR. GERMANY (17 B.C.)

RHAETIA (15 B.C.)

NORICUM (15 B.C.)

UPPER PANNONIA

Lugdunum

P

Aquileia

AQUITANIA

NARBONENSIS

C

M

I T A L Y

Adriatic Sea

Nemausus

Rome

TARRACONENSIS

Tarraco

LUSITANIA (c. 27 B.C.)

Naulochus

Corduba

SICILY

BAETICA

Carthage

Gades

Naval victory over Sextus Pompeius 36 B.C.

MAURETANIA

A F R I C A

──────── Imperial frontier as in A.D. 14

- - - - - Provincial frontiers

<u>ASIA</u> Senatorial provinces

<u>ALPINE PROVINCES</u> (15-14 B.C.)
M: Maritime, C: Cottian, P: Pennine

The hatched areas represent the more important dependent ('client') states, whose monarchs enjoyed internal autonomy but had to support Rome's foreign policy and help defend the imperial frontiers.

///// Principal client states

57

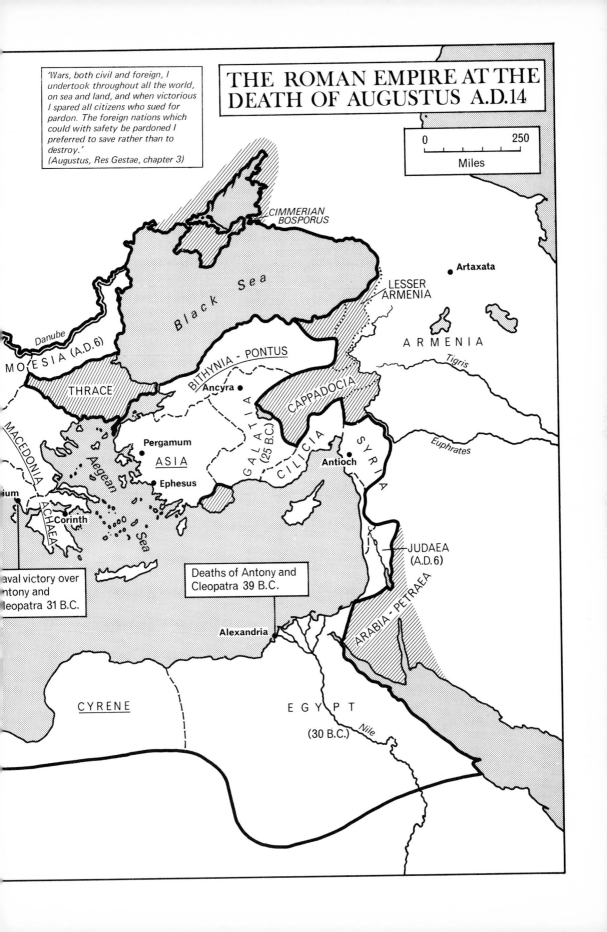

THE ROMAN EMPIRE AT THE
DEATH OF AUGUSTUS A.D.14

0   250

Miles

CIMMERIAN
BOSPORUS

• Artaxata

LESSER
ARMENIA

A R M E N I A

Black   Sea

Tigris

MO E S I A (A.D. 6)

Danube

BITHYNIA - PONTUS

Ancyra •

CAPPADOCIA

THRACE

GALATIA
(25 B.C.)

CILICIA

S
Y
R
I
A

Euphrates

MACEDONIA

Pergamum •

ASIA

Antioch •

Aegean

Ephesus •

JUDAEA
(A.D. 6)

ium

ACHAEA

Corinth •

Sea

A
R
A
B
I
A - PETRAEA

aval victory over
ntony and
leopatra 31 B.C.

Deaths of Antony and
Cleopatra 39 B.C.

Alexandria •

CYRENE

E G Y P T

(30 B.C.)

Nile

All roads lead to Rome: the most potent guarantees of external and internal peace and stimulants of prosperity.

Legend:
- Imperial frontier as in A.D. 14
- Roman roads
- Mountain contours

Map labels:
GAUL · SPAIN · AFRICA · ITALY · Rome

Rhine · Danube · Rhone · Ebro

Arelate · Narbo · Forum Julii

VIA DOMITIA

Adriatic Sea · Tyrrhenian Sea · Mediterranean

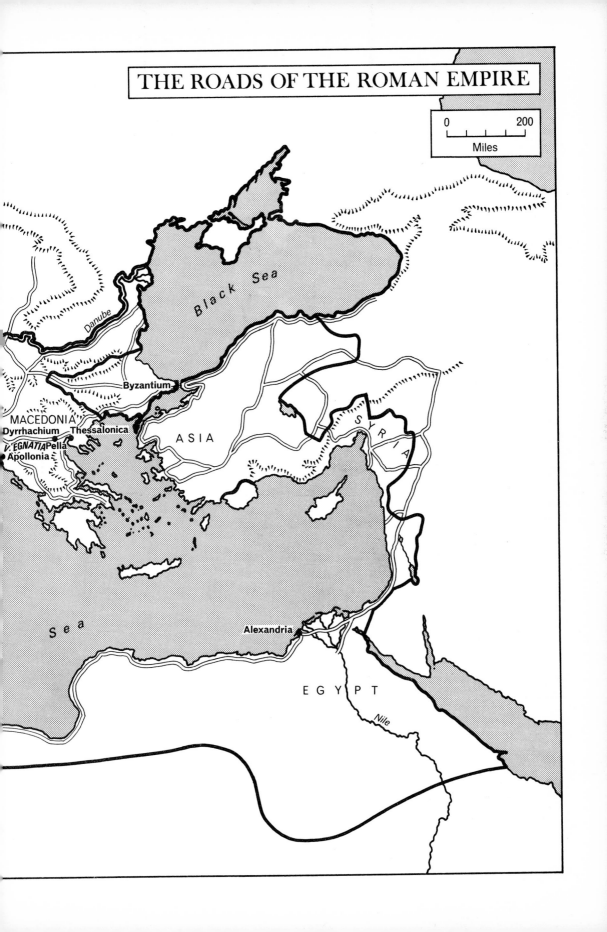

THE ROADS OF THE ROMAN EMPIRE

0   200
Miles

Danube

Black Sea

Byzantium

MACEDONIA
Dyrrhachium   **Thessalonica**
V. EGNATIA **Pella**
Apollonia

ASIA

S Y R I A

Sea

Alexandria

E G Y P T

Nile

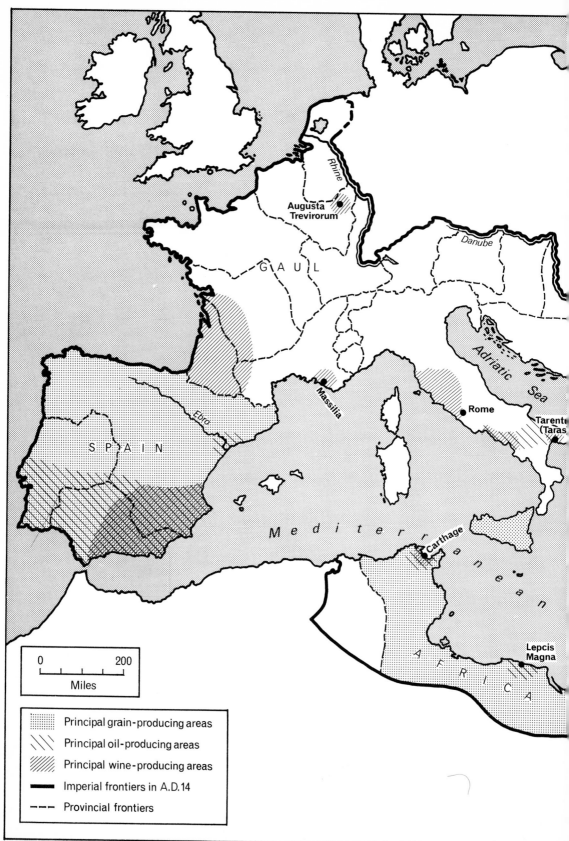

Rhine

Augusta
Trevirorum

G A U L

Danube

Adriatic Sea

Massilia

Rome

Tarent
(Taras

S P A I N

Ebro

M e d i t e r r a n e a n

Carthage

Lepcis
Magna

A F R I C A

```
0          200
 |    |    |    |    |
       Miles
```

▦ Principal grain-producing areas
▨ Principal oil-producing areas
▨ Principal wine-producing areas
━━ Imperial frontiers in A.D. 14
- - - Provincial frontiers

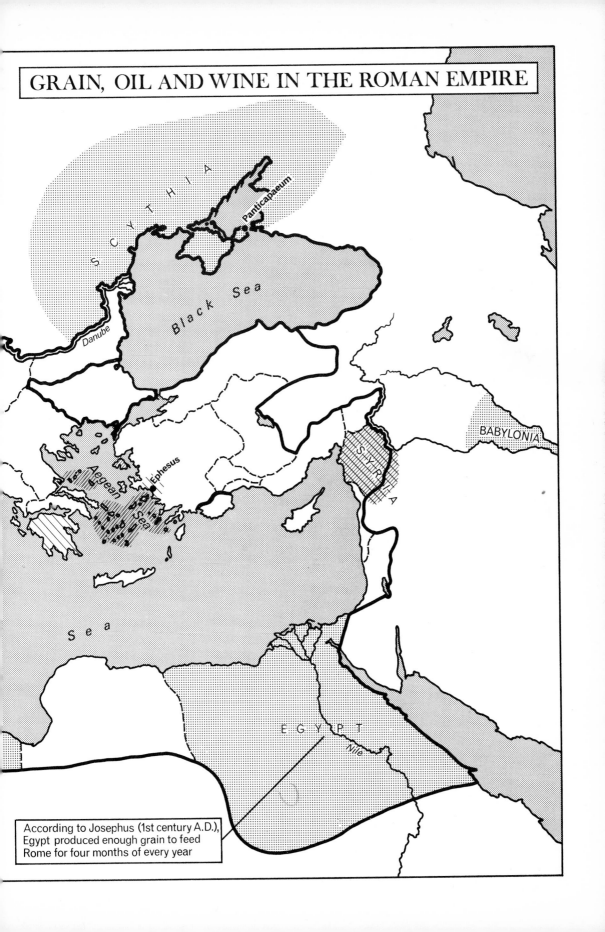

GRAIN, OIL AND WINE IN THE ROMAN EMPIRE

SCYTHIA

Panticapaeum

Black Sea

Danube

BABYLONIA

SYRIA

Aegean Sea

Ephesus

Sea

EGYPT

Nile

According to Josephus (1st century A.D.), Egypt produced enough grain to feed Rome for four months of every year

BRITAIN

TIN IRON LEAD
COPPER WOOL
HIDES

AMBER HIDES HORSES
LEATHER

FREE GERMANY

GLASS
METALS
WOOL

Rhine

WINE
POTTERY

Danube

GAUL

GOLD SILVER IRON
POTTERY GLASS
WINE OIL WOOL
LINEN MARBLE

GOLD
IRON

METALS
HIDES

Rhone

GOLD
SILVE
IRON
TIMB

I T A L Y

Ebro

GOLD SILVER IRON
COPPER TIN LEAD
FRUIT WINE HORSES
MARBLE LINEN
POTTERY

GRAIN

SARDINIA

IRON WINE OIL
GLASS POTTERY
MARBLE WOOL
LINEN

Guadiana S P A I N

GRAIN FRUIT
WOOL SULPHUR

MAURETANIA

NUMIDIA

A F R I C A

MARBLE WOOL
POTTERY IVORY
OSTRICHES

TIMBER
WILD ANIMALS

Imperial frontier in A.D.14

0   200

Miles

'Now indeed it is possible for Hellene
or non-Hellene, with or without his
property, to travel wherever he will,
easily, just as if passing from fatherland to fatherland.' (Aelius Aristides
of Hadrianotherae in Asia Minor,
2nd century AD, Roman Oration,
94, translated by J.H. Oliver).

GRAIN OIL POTTERY
MARBLE PURPLE-DYE
WOOL WILD ANIMALS

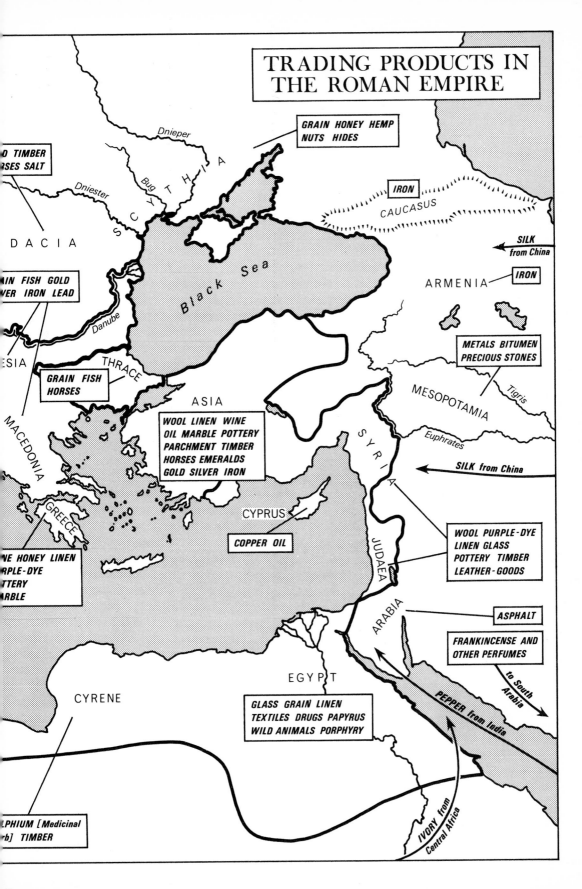

TRADING PRODUCTS IN THE ROMAN EMPIRE

Dnieper

GRAIN HONEY HEMP NUTS HIDES

Bug

S C Y T H I A

Dniester

IRON

CAUCASUS

D TIMBER
SES SALT

SILK
from China

D A C I A

ARMENIA — **IRON**

Black Sea

IN FISH GOLD
ER IRON LEAD

Danube

METALS BITUMEN PRECIOUS STONES

Tigris

ESIA

THRACE

MESOPOTAMIA

GRAIN FISH HORSES

Euphrates

ASIA

S Y R I A

SILK from China

MACEDONIA

WOOL LINEN WINE OIL MARBLE POTTERY PARCHMENT TIMBER HORSES EMERALDS GOLD SILVER IRON

GREECE

CYPRUS

JUDAEA

WOOL PURPLE-DYE LINEN GLASS POTTERY TIMBER LEATHER-GOODS

NE HONEY LINEN
RPLE-DYE
TTERY
RBLE

COPPER OIL

ARABIA

ASPHALT

FRANKINCENSE AND OTHER PERFUMES

to South Arabia

EGYPT

CYRENE

GLASS GRAIN LINEN TEXTILES DRUGS PAPYRUS WILD ANIMALS PORPHYRY

PEPPER from India

LPHIUM [Medicinal
rb] TIMBER

IVORY from Central Africa

F

Major mints. Date at which Rome
supersedes Lugdunum uncertain.
Designs of copper, and perhaps
for a time silver coins, imitated at
many other mints.

BELGICA

LUGDUNENSIS

RHAETIA

NORICUM

G A U L

Lugdunum
♦ □ ■ ▲

Extensive bronze city-
coinages cease under
Caligula (A.D. 37 - 41)

AQUITANIA

I

T

NARBONENSIS

Nemausus
○

ILLYRICU

A

TARRACONENSIS

Large temporary
city-coinage
circulates through-
out west

L

Y

Rome
■ ▲ □ ♦

SPAIN
○

LUSITANIA

BAETICA

NUMIDIA

A F R I C A
○

■ Gold
▲ Silver
△ Base silver
□ Brass
○ Bronze
♦ Copper

Note: Augustus reformed and enlarged the
Roman imperial coinage, issuing gold, silver,
brass and copper on an enormous scale

Small bronze city-coinage
virtually cease under
Tiberius (A.D. 14)

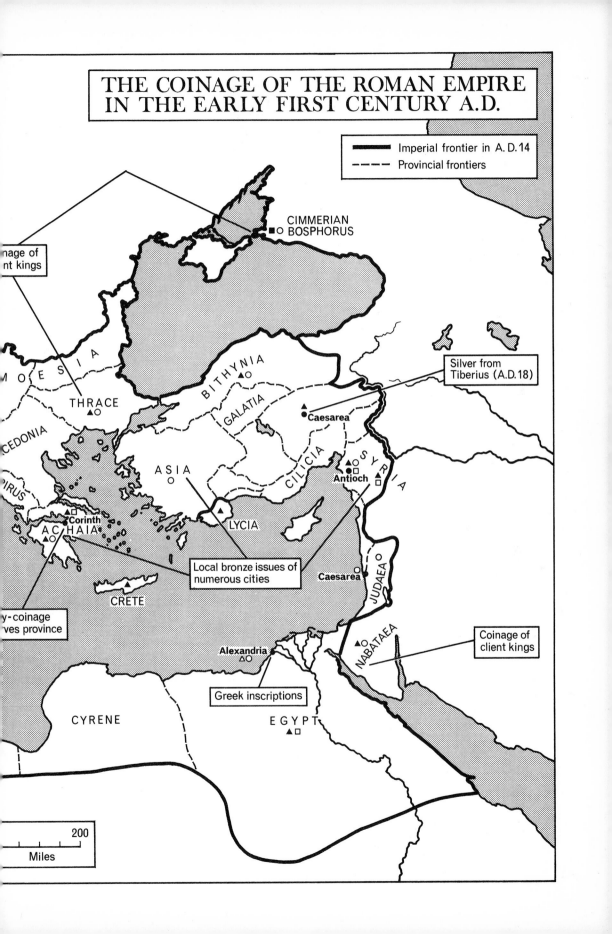

THE COINAGE OF THE ROMAN EMPIRE
IN THE EARLY FIRST CENTURY A.D.

Imperial frontier in A.D.14
Provincial frontiers

CIMMERIAN
BOSPHORUS

...nage of
...nt kings

MOESIA

THRACE

...CEDONIA

...PIRUS

ACHAIA

Corinth

BITHYNIA

GALATIA

ASIA

LYCIA

CILICIA

Caesarea

Silver from
Tiberius (A.D.18)

SYRIA

Antioch

Local bronze issues of
numerous cities

CRETE

Caesarea

JUDAEA

...y-coinage
...ves province

Alexandria

NABATAEA

Coinage of
client kings

Greek inscriptions

CYRENE

EGYPT

200

Miles

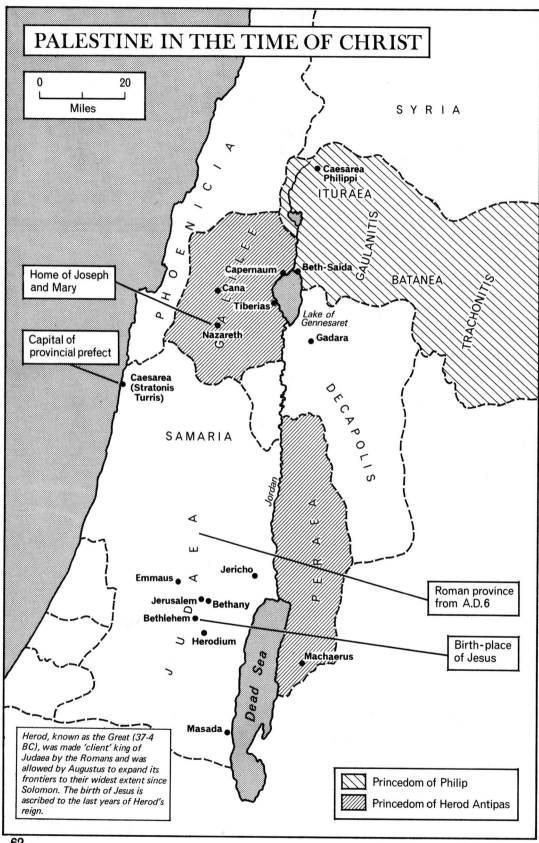

PALESTINE IN THE TIME OF CHRIST

0   20
Miles

SYRIA

PHOENICIA

● Caesarea
Philippi

ITURAEA

GAULANITIS

BATANEA

TRACHONITIS

Home of Joseph
and Mary

Capernaum ●

● Cana

Beth-Saida

Tiberias

GALILEE

Lake of
Gennesaret

Capital of
provincial prefect

● Nazareth

● Gadara

DECAPOLIS

Caesarea
(Stratonis
Turris) ●

SAMARIA

Jordan

PERAEA

Roman province
from A.D. 6

Emmaus ●

Jericho ●

JUDAEA

Jerusalem ●● Bethany

Bethlehem ●

Birth-place
of Jesus

‿ Herodium

Dead Sea

● Machaerus

● Masada

*Herod, known as the Great (37-4
BC), was made 'client' king of
Judaea by the Romans and was
allowed by Augustus to expand its
frontiers to their widest extent since
Solomon. The birth of Jesus is
ascribed to the last years of Herod's
reign.*

Princedom of Philip

Princedom of Herod Antipas

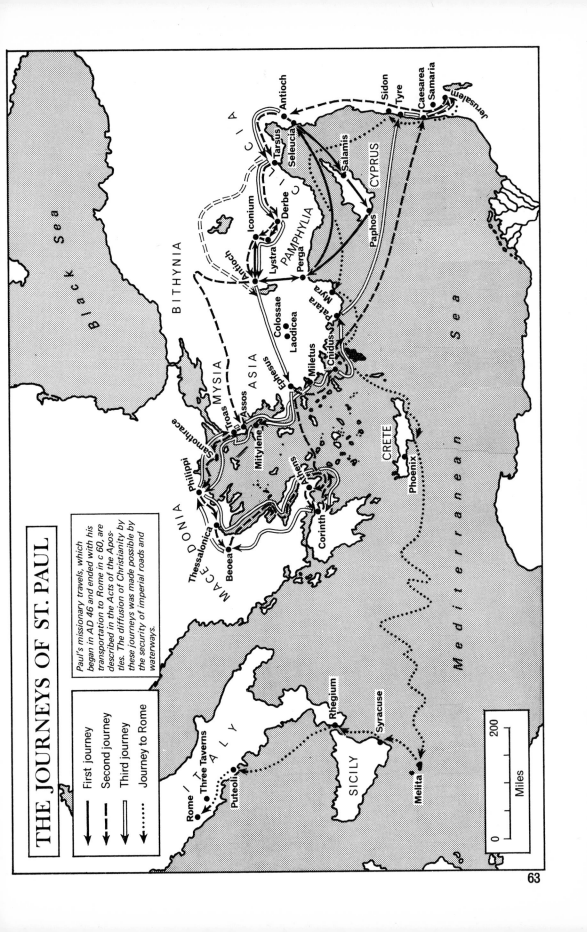

THE JOURNEYS OF ST. PAUL

Paul's missionary travels, which began in AD 46 and ended with his transportation to Rome in c 60, are described in the Acts of the Apostles. The diffusion of Christianity by these journeys was made possible by the security of imperial roads and waterways.

First journey
Second journey
Third journey
Journey to Rome

Black Sea

Mediterranean Sea

BITHYNIA

MYSIA

ASIA

MACEDONIA

Thessalonica
Beoea
Philippi
Samothrace
Athens
Corinth
Troas
Assos
Mitylene
Ephesus
Miletus
Cnidus
Laodicea
Colossae
Patara
Myra
Perga
PAMPHYLIA
Antioch
Lystra
Derbe
Iconium
Tarsus
Seleucia
Antioch
Salamis
CYPRUS
Paphos
Sidon
Tyre
Caesarea
Samaria
Jerusalem

CRETE
Phoenix

ITALY
Rome
Three Taverns
Puteoli
Rhegium
Syracuse
SICILY
Melita

200
Miles
0

63

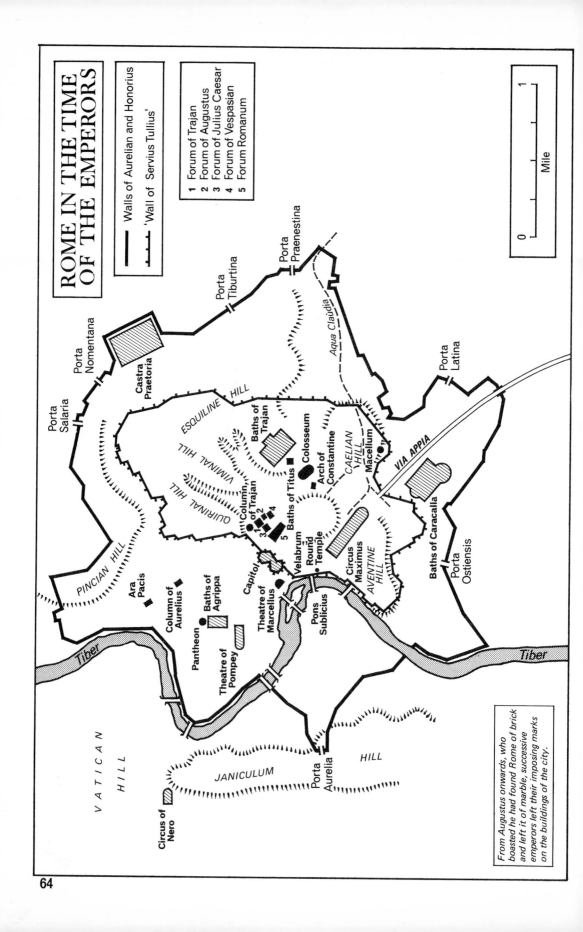

ROME IN THE TIME OF THE EMPERORS

—— Walls of Aurelian and Honorius

····· 'Wall of Servius Tullius'

1 Forum of Trajan
2 Forum of Augustus
3 Forum of Julius Caesar
4 Forum of Vespasian
5 Forum Romanum

0   Mile   1

Porta Praenestina

Porta Tiburtina

Aqua Claudia

Porta Latina

Porta Nomentana

Castra Praetoria

Porta Salaria

ESQUILINE HILL

Baths of Trajan

Colosseum

Arch of Constantine

CAELIAN HILL

Macellum

VIMINAL HILL

QUIRINAL HILL

Column of Trajan

Baths of Titus

2

4

VIA APPIA

3

1

5

PINCIAN HILL

Velabrum

Round Temple

Circus Maximus

AVENTINE HILL

Baths of Caracalla

Porta Ostiensis

Ara Pacis

Column of Aurelius

Pantheon

Baths of Agrippa

Capitol

Theatre of Marcellus

Pons Sublicius

Theatre of Pompey

Tiber

Tiber

VATICAN HILL

Circus of Nero

JANICULUM

Porta Aurelia

HILL

From Augustus onwards, who boasted he had found Rome of brick and left it of marble, successive emperors left their imposing marks on the buildings of the city.

64

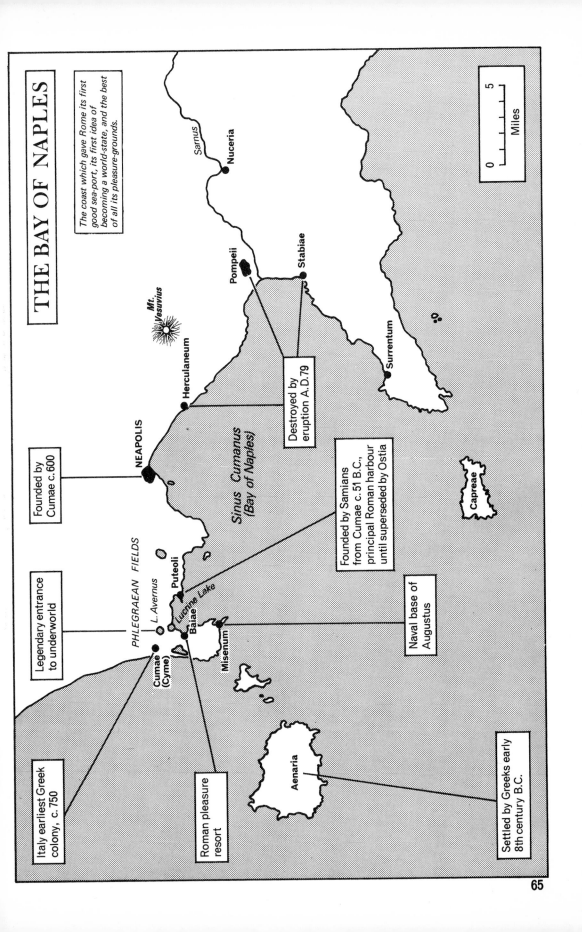

THE BAY OF NAPLES

The coast which gave Rome its first good sea-port, its first idea of becoming a world-state, and the best of all its pleasure-grounds.

Sarnus

Nuceria

Stabiae

Pompeii

Surrentum

Mt. Vesuvius

Herculaneum

NEAPOLIS

Sinus Cumanus (Bay of Naples)

Founded by Cumae c.600

Destroyed by eruption A.D.79

Founded by Samians from Cumae c.51 B.C., principal Roman harbour until superseded by Ostia

Naval base of Augustus

Capreae

PHLEGRAEAN FIELDS

L. Avernus

Puteoli

Lucrine Lake

Baiae

Misenum

Cumae (Cyme)

Legendary entrance to underworld

Italy earliest Greek colony, c.750

Roman pleasure resort

Aenaria

Settled by Greeks early 8th century B.C.

Miles

0   5

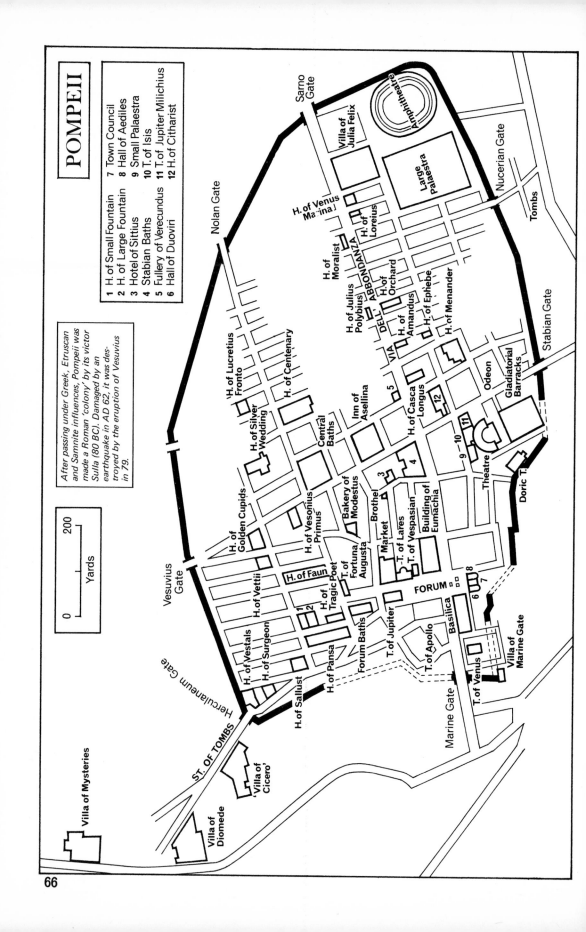

POMPEII

1 H. of Small Fountain
2 H. of Large Fountain
3 Hotel of Sittius
4 Stabian Baths
5 Fullery of Verecundus
6 Hall of Duoviri
7 Town Council
8 Hall of Aediles
9 Small Palaestra
10 T. of Isis
11 T. of Jupiter Milichius
12 H. of Citharist

After passing under Greek, Etruscan and Samnite influences, Pompeii was made a Roman 'colony' by its victor Sulla (80 BC). Damaged by an earthquake in AD 62, it was destroyed by the eruption of Vesuvius in 79.

0   200
Yards

Sarno Gate

Amphitheatre

Villa of Julia Felix

Nucerian Gate

Large Palaestra

H. of Venus Marina

Tombs

H. of Moralist

H. of Loreius

DELL' ABBONDANZA

H. of Orchard

VIA

H. of Amandus

H. of Ephebe

H. of Menander

Nolan Gate

H. of Julius Polybius

H. of Lucretius Fronto

H. of Centenary

Inn of Asellina

5

H. of Casca Longus

12

Stabian Gate

H. of Silver Wedding

Central Baths

Odeon

Gladiatorial Barracks

H. of Golden Cupids

Bakery of Modestus

3

4

11

9 10

9–10

Theatre

Doric T.

H. of Vesonius Primus

Brothel

Market

T. of Lares

T. of Vespasian

Building of Eumachia

H. of Vettii

H. of Faun

T. of Fortuna Augusta

1

2

H. of Tragic Poet

FORUM

8

7

6

Villa of Marine Gate

H. of Vestals

H. of Surgeon

H. of Pansa

Forum Baths

T. of Jupiter

Basilica

T. of Apollo

T. of Venus

Vesuvius Gate

H. of Sallust

Herculaneum Gate

Marine Gate

ST. OF TOMBS

'Villa of Cicero'

Villa of Diomede

Villa of Mysteries

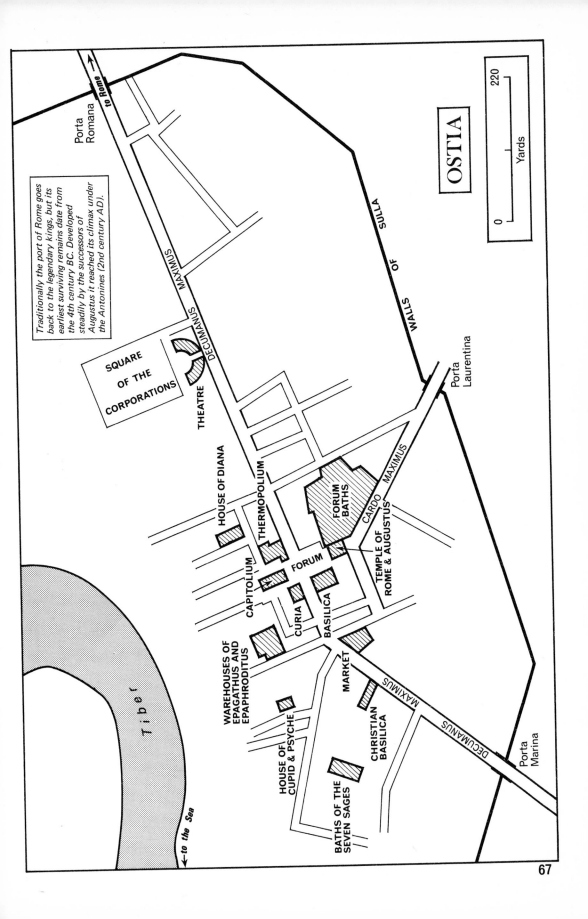

OSTIA

Yards
0   220

Traditionally the port of Rome goes back to the legendary kings, but its earliest surviving remains date from the 4th century BC. Developed steadily by the successors of Augustus it reached its climax under the Antonines (2nd century AD).

Porta Romana

to Rome →

SQUARE OF THE CORPORATIONS

THEATRE

DECUMANUS MAXIMUS

HOUSE OF DIANA

THERMOPOLIUM

CAPITOLIUM

FORUM

CURIA

BASILICA

FORUM BATHS

TEMPLE OF ROME & AUGUSTUS

CARDO MAXIMUS

WALLS OF SULLA

Porta Laurentina

WAREHOUSES OF EPAGATHUS AND EPAPHRODITUS

HOUSE OF CUPID & PSYCHE

MARKET

CHRISTIAN BASILICA

BATHS OF THE SEVEN SAGES

DECUMANUS MAXIMUS

Porta Marina

Tiber

to the Sea →

67

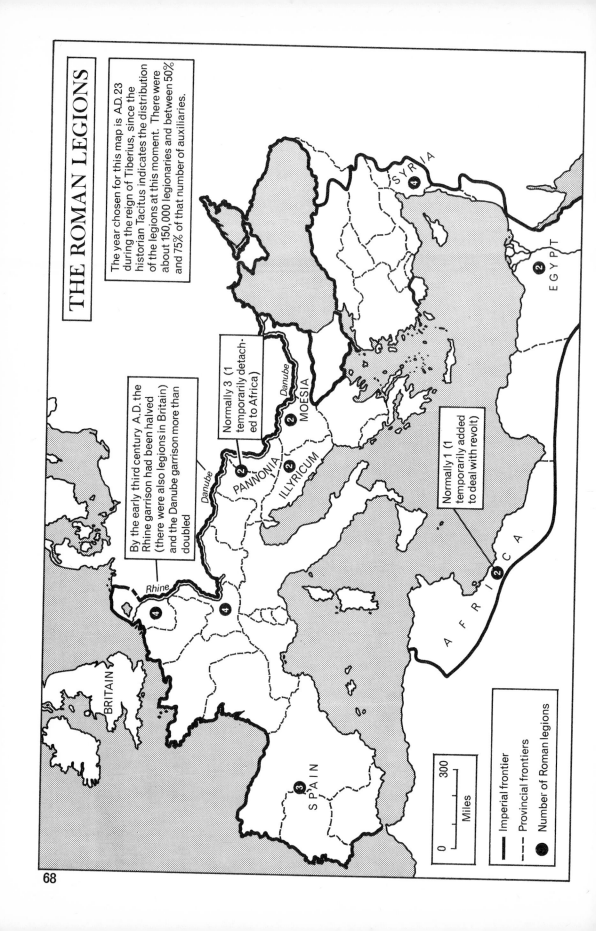

THE ROMAN LEGIONS

The year chosen for this map is A.D. 23 during the reign of Tiberius, since the historian Tacitus indicates the distribution of the legions at this moment. There were about 150,000 legionaries and between 50% and 75% of that number of auxiliaries.

By the early third century A.D. the Rhine garrison had been halved (there were also legions in Britain) and the Danube garrison more than doubled

Normally 3 (1 temporarily detach-ed to Africa)

Normally 1 (1 temporarily added to deal with revolt)

BRITAIN

Rhine

SPAIN

AFRICA

EGYPT

SYRIA

PANNONIA

ILLYRICUM

MOESIA

Danube

Danube

Imperial frontier
Provincial frontiers
Number of Roman legions

0   300
Miles

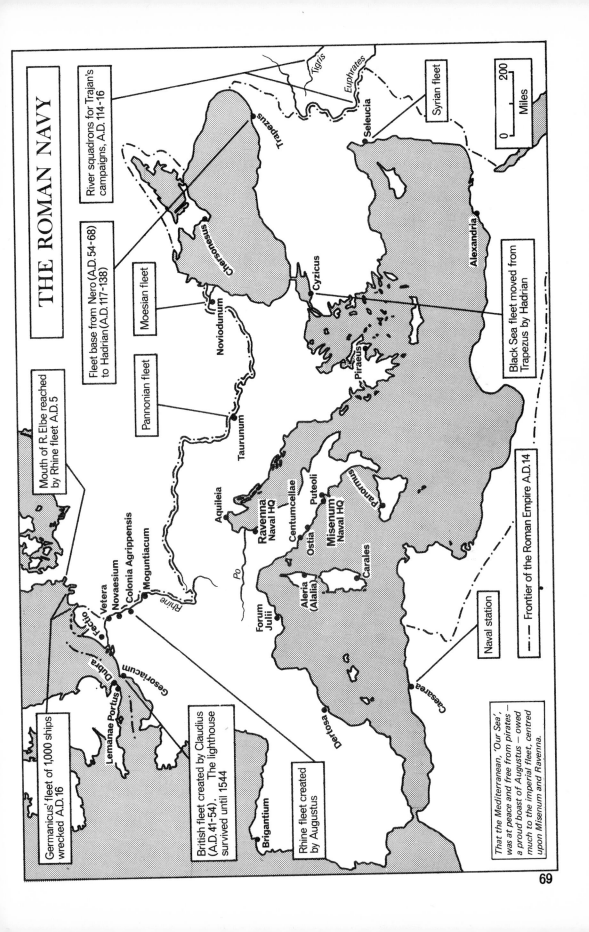

THE ROMAN NAVY

River squadrons for Trajan's campaigns, A.D. 114-16

Fleet base from Nero (A.D. 54-68) to Hadrian (A.D. 117-138)

Moesian fleet

Pannonian fleet

Mouth of R. Elbe reached by Rhine fleet A.D.5

Germanicus' fleet of 1,000 ships wrecked A.D.16

British fleet created by Claudius (A.D. 41-54). The lighthouse survived until 1544

Rhine fleet created by Augustus

Syrian fleet

Black Sea fleet moved from Trapezus by Hadrian

Naval station

·—·—· Frontier of the Roman Empire A.D.14

That the Mediterranean, 'Our Sea', was at peace and free from pirates — a proud boast of Augustus — owed much to the imperial fleet, centred upon Misenum and Ravenna.

0   200
Miles

Seleucia

Alexandria

Trapezus

Chersonesus

Noviodunum

Taurunum

Cyzicus

Piraeus

Aquileia

Ravenna Naval HQ

Centumcellae

Puteoli

Ostia

Misenum Naval HQ

Pannonius

Carales

Forum Julii

Aleria (Alalia)

Dertosa

Caesarea

Vetera

Novaesium

Colonia Agrippensis

Moguntiacum

Rhine

Po

Fectio

Gesoriacum

Dubra

Lemanae Portus

Brigantium

Tigris

Euphrates

69

BRITANNIA (AD 71)
(AD 59)
(AD 43-47)
Londinium

FREE GERMANY

LOWER GERMANY
Colonia Agrippinensis

Rhine

AGRI DECUMAT. (83)
Moguntiacum

LUGDUNENSIS

UPPER GERMANY

RHAETIA

NORICUM

Danube

PANNONIA

UPPER

LOWER

GALLIA

AQUITANIA

Lugdunum

NARBONENSIS

ILLYRICUM

Aquileia

I
T
A
L
I
A

Adriatic Sea

Nemausus

TARRACONENSIS

Tarraco

HISPANIA

LUSITANIA

BAETICA

Corduba

Gades

Rome

SARDINIA

SICILY

Carthage

MAURETANIA (A.D. 42)

A F R I C A

‐ ‐ ‐	Frontier of Roman Empire A.D. 14
‐·‐·‐	Frontier of Roman Empire A.D. 117
·········	Province boundaries

70

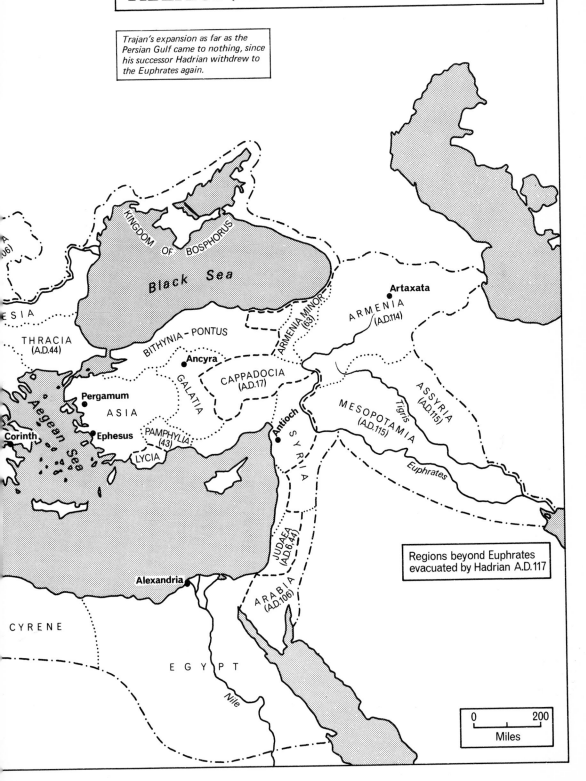

THE ROMAN EMPIRE FROM TIBERIUS (A.D.14-37) TO TRAJAN (98-117)

Trajan's expansion as far as the Persian Gulf came to nothing, since his successor Hadrian withdrew to the Euphrates again.

KINGDOM OF BOSPHORUS

Black Sea

Artaxata

ARMENIA MINOR (63)

ARMENIA (A.D.114)

ASIA

THRACIA (A.D.44)

BITHYNIA – PONTUS

ASSYRIA (A.D.115)

Ancyra

CAPPADOCIA (A.D.17)

GALATIA

MESOPOTAMIA (A.D.115)

Tigris

Pergamum

ASIA

Antioch

Corinth

Ephesus

PAMPHYLIA (43)

SYRIA

Euphrates

LYCIA

JUDAEA (A.D.6,44)

Aegean Sea

Regions beyond Euphrates evacuated by Hadrian A.D.117

Alexandria

ARABIA (A.D.106)

CYRENE

EGYPT

Nile

0   200
Miles

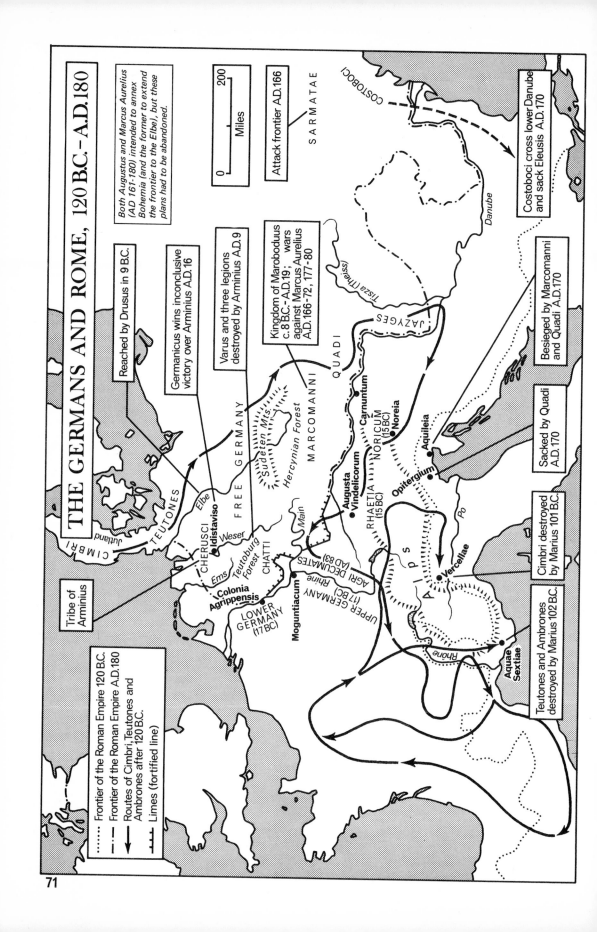

THE GERMANS AND ROME, 120 B.C.–A.D.180

Both Augustus and Marcus Aurelius (AD 161-180) intended to annex Bohemia (and the former to extend the frontier to the Elbe), but these plans had to be abandoned.

Reached by Drusus in 9 B.C.

Germanicus wins inconclusive victory over Arminius A.D.16

Varus and three legions destroyed by Arminius A.D.9

Kingdom of Maroboduus c.8 B.C.–A.D.19; wars against Marcus Aurelius A.D.166-72, 177-80

Attack frontier A.D.166

Costoboci cross lower Danube and sack Eleusis A.D.170

Besieged by Marcomanni and Quadi A.D.170

Sacked by Quadi A.D.170

Cimbri destroyed by Marius 101 B.C.

Teutones and Ambrones destroyed by Marius 102 B.C.

Tribe of Arminius

200

0

Miles

SARMATAE

COSTOBOCI

Danube

Tisza (Tibiss)

JAZYGES

QUADI

MARCOMANNI

Hercynian Forest

Sudeten Mts.

FREE GERMANY

Elbe

Idistaviso

Weser

CHERUSCI

Ems

Teutoburg Forest

CHATTI

Main

Colonia Agrippensis

Moguntiacum

LOWER GERMANY (17 BC)

UPPER GERMANY (17 BC)

AGRI DECUMATES (AD 83)

Rhine

RHAETIA (15 BC)

Augusta Vindelicorum

NORICUM (15 BC)

Carnuntum

Noreia

Aquileia

Opitergium

A L P S

Vercellae

Rhone

Aquae Sextiae

Po

TEUTONES

CIMBRI

Jutland

— Frontier of the Roman Empire 120 B.C.
— Frontier of the Roman Empire A.D.180
— Routes of Cimbri, Teutones and Ambrones after 120 B.C.
— Limes (fortified line)

71

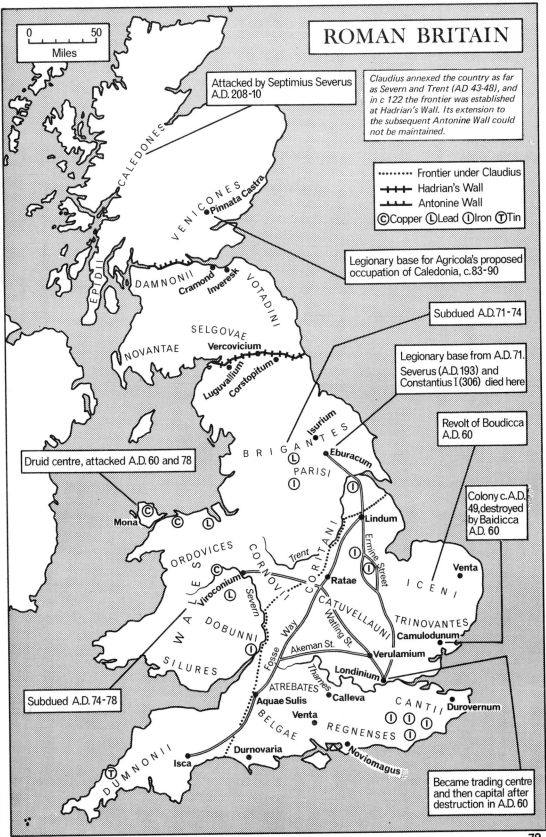

ROMAN BRITAIN

Attacked by Septimius Severus
A.D. 208-10

Claudius annexed the country as far as Severn and Trent (AD 43-48), and in c 122 the frontier was established at Hadrian's Wall. Its extension to the subsequent Antonine Wall could not be maintained.

.... Frontier under Claudius
+++ Hadrian's Wall
⊥⊥⊥ Antonine Wall
©Copper ⓁLead ⒾIron ⓉTin

Legionary base for Agricola's proposed occupation of Caledonia, c.83-90

Subdued A.D. 71-74

Legionary base from A.D. 71. Severus (A.D. 193) and Constantius I (306) died here

Revolt of Boudicca A.D. 60

Druid centre, attacked A.D. 60 and 78

Colony c.A.D. 49, destroyed by Baidicca A.D. 60

Subdued A.D. 74-78

Became trading centre and then capital after destruction in A.D. 60

CALEDONES

VENICONES

Pinnata Castra

EPTDII

DAMNONII

Cramond Inveresk

VOTADINI

SELGOVAE

Vercovicium

NOVANTAE

Luguvallium Corstopitum

BRIGANTES

Isurium

PARISI

Eburacum

Mona © © Ⓛ

ORDOVICES

CORNOVII

Ⓛ

Lindum

Ⓘ

Ⓘ

Ⓘ

Venta

ICENI

©

Viroconium

Ⓛ

Trent

CORITANI

Ratae

Ⓘ

Ⓘ

Severn

CATUVELLAUNI

TRINOVANTES

W
A
L
E
S

DOBUNNI

Ⓘ

SILURES

Fosse Way

Akeman St.

Watling St.

Camulodunum

Verulamium

Thames

Londinium

ATREBATES

Aquae Sulis

Calleva

CANTII

BELGAE

Venta

REGNENSES

Ⓘ Ⓘ Ⓘ

Durovernum

Ⓘ

Ⓘ

DUMNONII

Durnovaria

Ⓣ

Isca

Noviomagus

Ermine Street

0   50
Miles

72

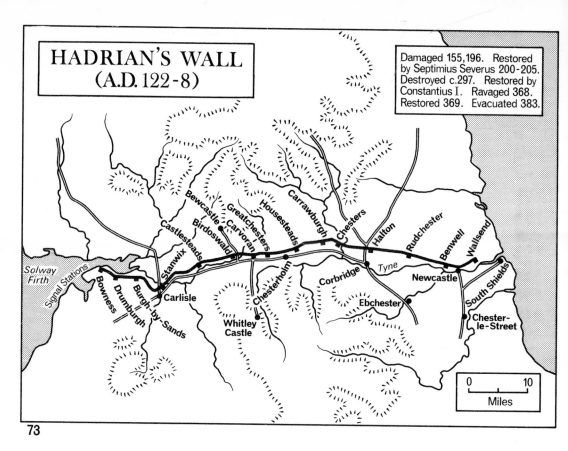

HADRIAN'S WALL
(A.D. 122-8)

Damaged 155,196. Restored by Septimius Severus 200-205. Destroyed c.297. Restored by Constantius I. Ravaged 368. Restored 369. Evacuated 383.

Bewcastle

Greatchesters

Housesteads

Carrawburgh

Chesters

Halton

Rudchester

Benwell

Wallsend

Castlesteads

Birdoswald

Carvoran

Castlesteads

Stanwix

Solway Firth

Signal Stations

Bowness

Drumburgh

Burgh-by-Sands

Carlisle

Chesterholm

Corbridge

Tyne

Newcastle

South Shields

Ebchester

Whitley Castle

Chester-le-Street

0   10
Miles

73

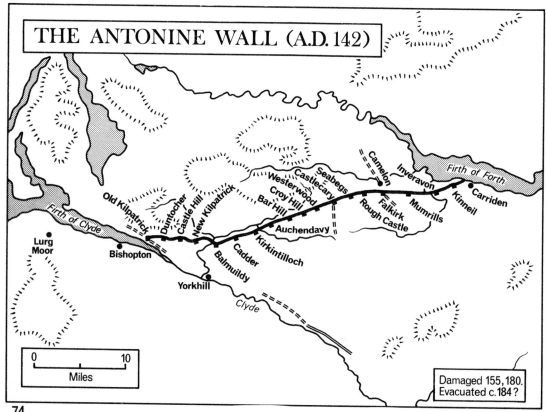

THE ANTONINE WALL (A.D. 142)

Firth of Forth

Cramon

Inveravon

Carriden

Seabegs

Castlecary

Westerwood

Croy Hill

Bar Hill

Falkirk

Mumrills

Kinneil

Old Kilpatrick

Duntocher

Castle Hill

New Kilpatrick

Rough Castle

Firth of Clyde

Auchendavy

Lurg Moor

Bishopton

Cadder

Kirkintilloch

Balmuildy

Yorkhill

Clyde

0   10
Miles

Damaged 155, 180. Evacuated c. 184 ?

74

THE WORLD ACCORDING TO PTOLEMY, c. A.D. 150

The Geography of Claudius Ptolemaeus of Alexandria, including an atlas, showed awareness of the existence of China, but not of its shape.

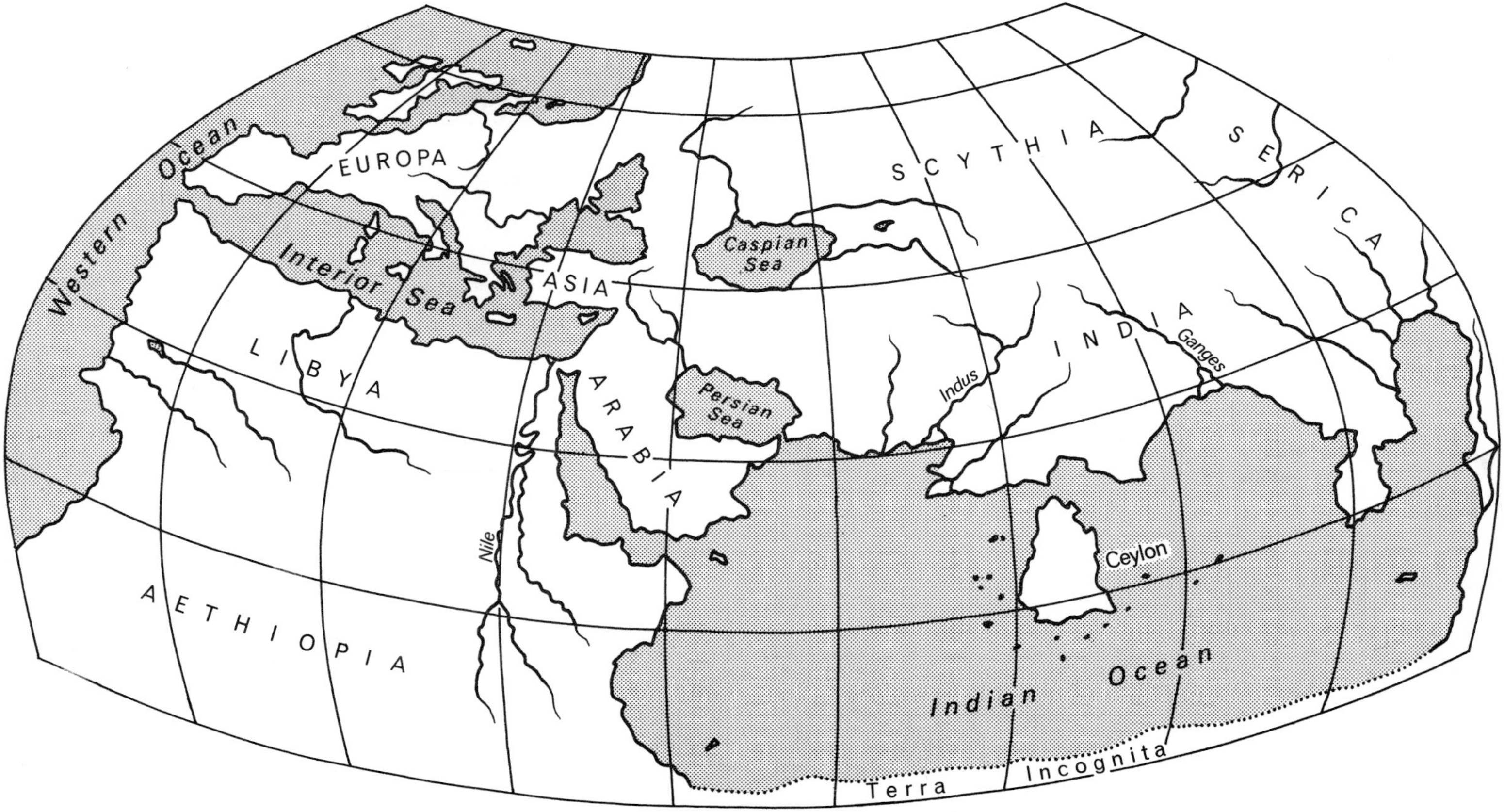

SERICA

SCYTHIA

INDIA

Ganges

Indus

Ceylon

Indian Ocean

Terra Incognita

Caspian Sea

Persian Sea

ARABIA

ASIA

EUROPA

Interior Sea

LIBYA

Nile

AETHIOPIA

Western Ocean

G

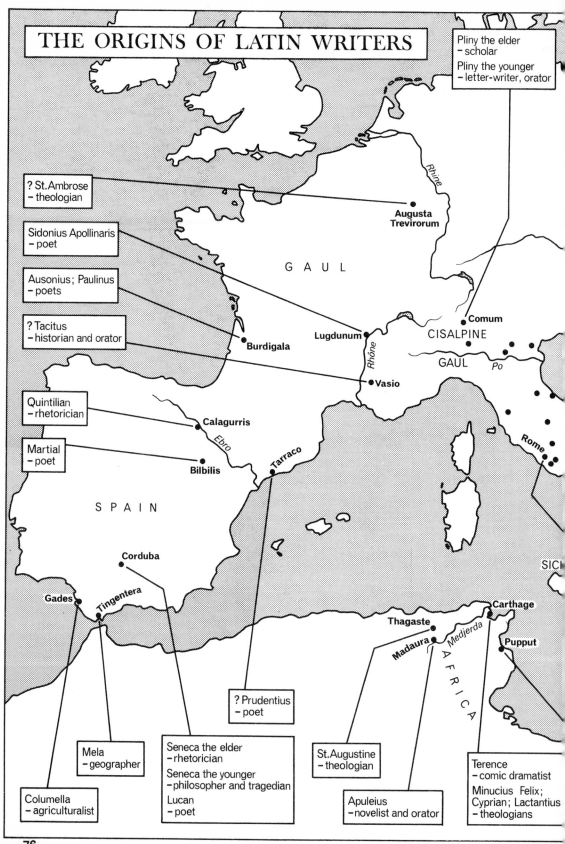

THE ORIGINS OF LATIN WRITERS

Pliny the elder
– scholar

Pliny the younger
– letter-writer, orator

? St.Ambrose
– theologian

Sidonius Apollinaris
– poet

Ausonius; Paulinus
– poets

? Tacitus
– historian and orator

Quintilian
– rhetorician

Martial
– poet

Mela
– geographer

Columella
– agriculturalist

? Prudentius
– poet

Seneca the elder
– rhetorician

Seneca the younger
– philosopher and tragedian

Lucan
– poet

St.Augustine
– theologian

Apuleius
– novelist and orator

Terence
– comic dramatist

Minucius Felix;
Cyprian; Lactantius
– theologians

GAUL

Rhine

Augusta
Trevirorum

Comum

CISALPINE

GAUL

Po

Lugdunum

Rhône

Vasio

Burdigala

Calagurris

Ebro

Tarraco

Bilbilis

Rome

SPAIN

Corduba

SICI

Gades

Tingentera

Carthage

Thagaste

Medjerda

Pupput

Madaura

AFRICA

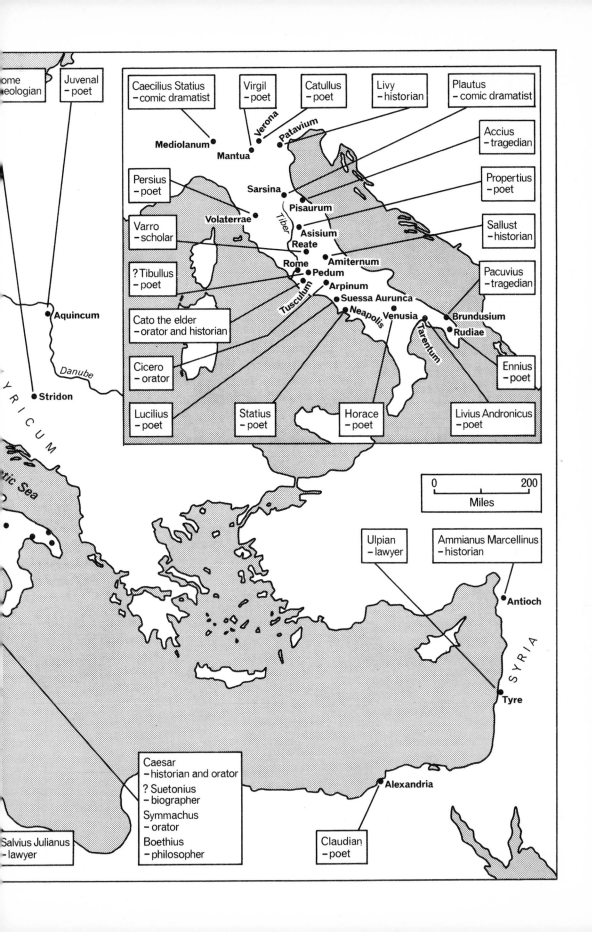

Rome
theologian

Juvenal
– poet

Caecilius Statius
– comic dramatist

Virgil
– poet

Catullus
– poet

Livy
– historian

Plautus
– comic dramatist

Verona

Patavium

Mediolanum

Mantua

Accius
– tragedian

Persius
– poet

Sarsina

Propertius
– poet

Pisaurum

Volaterrae

Tiber

Asisium

Reate

Amiternum

Sallust
– historian

Varro
– scholar

Rome

Pedum

? Tibullus
– poet

Arpinum

Pacuvius
– tragedian

Suessa Aurunca

Tusculum

Neapolis

Venusia

Brundusium

Cato the elder
– orator and historian

Tarentum

Rudiae

Aquincum

Cicero
– orator

Ennius
– poet

ILLYRICUM

Stridon

Danube

Lucilius
– poet

Statius
– poet

Horace
– poet

Livius Andronicus
– poet

Adriatic Sea

0   200
Miles

Ulpian
– lawyer

Ammianus Marcellinus
– historian

Antioch

SYRIA

Tyre

Caesar
– historian and orator

? Suetonius
– biographer

Symmachus
– orator

Boethius
– philosopher

Salvius Julianus
– lawyer

Claudian
– poet

Alexandria

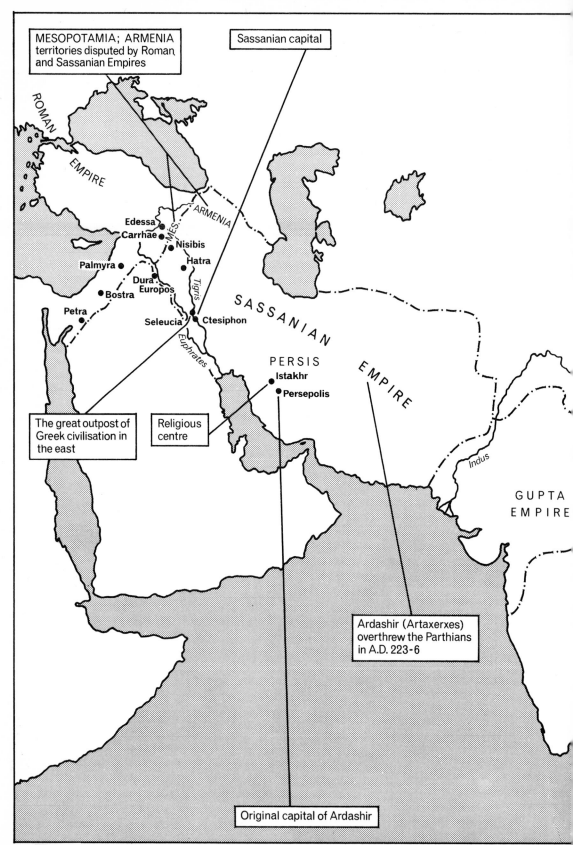

MESOPOTAMIA; ARMENIA
territories disputed by Roman
and Sassanian Empires

Sassanian capital

ROMAN

EMPIRE

ARMENIA

Edessa
Carrhae
Nisibis
Hatra
Palmyra
Dura
Europos
Bostra
Petra
Seleucia Ctesiphon

MES.

Tigris

Euphrates

SASSANIAN

EMPIRE

PERSIS
Istakhr
Persepolis

The great outpost of
Greek civilisation in
the east

Religious
centre

Indus

GUPTA
EMPIRE

Ardashir (Artaxerxes)
overthrew the Parthians
in A.D. 223-6

Original capital of Ardashir

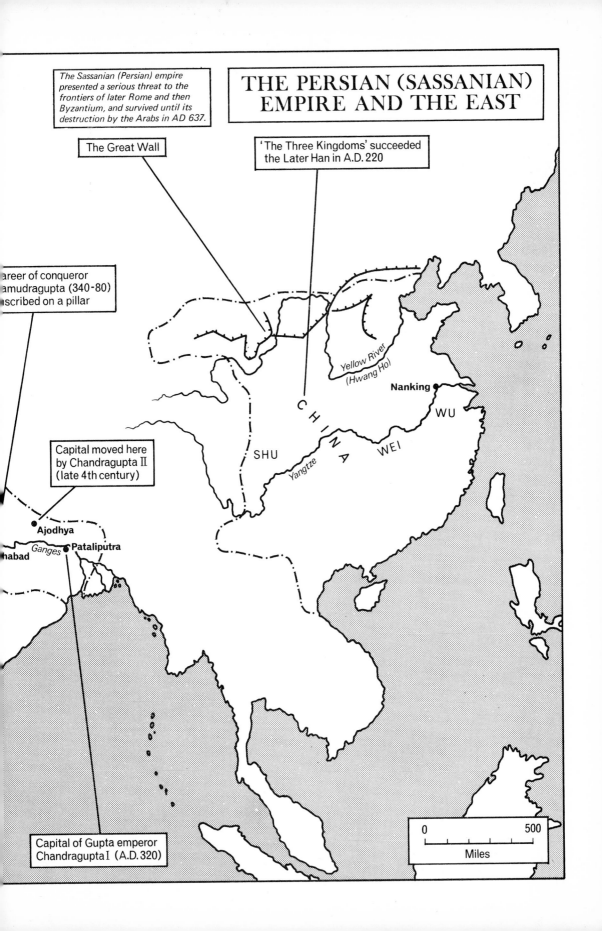

The Sassanian (Persian) empire presented a serious threat to the frontiers of later Rome and then Byzantium, and survived until its destruction by the Arabs in AD 637.

THE PERSIAN (SASSANIAN) EMPIRE AND THE EAST

The Great Wall

'The Three Kingdoms' succeeded the Later Han in A.D. 220

areer of conqueror amudragupta (340-80) scribed on a pillar

Yellow River (Hwang Ho)

Nanking

C H I N A

WU

WEI

SHU

Yangtze

Capital moved here by Chandragupta II (late 4th century)

Ajodhya

Ganges   Pataliputra

habad

Capital of Gupta emperor Chandragupta I (A.D. 320)

0   500

Miles

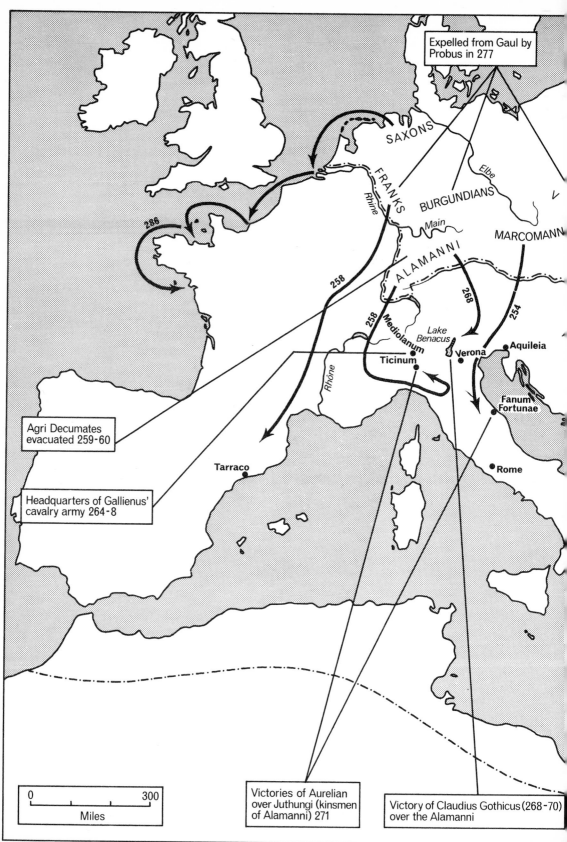

Expelled from Gaul by Probus in 277

SAXONS

FRANKS

BURGUNDIANS

Elbe

MARCOMANN

Main

ALAMANNI

Rhine

286

258

258

268

254

Mediolanum

Lake Benacus

Ticinum

Verona

Aquileia

Rhône

Fanum Fortunae

Agri Decumates evacuated 259-60

Tarraco

Rome

Headquarters of Gallienus' cavalry army 264-8

0   300
Miles

Victories of Aurelian over Juthungi (kinsmen of Alamanni) 271

Victory of Claudius Gothicus (268-70) over the Alamanni

GERMAN INVASIONS IN THE THIRD CENTURY A.D.

From the 230s until the 260s the Germans burst over the frontiers with ever increasing force, but then the dissolution of the empire was prevented by Gallienus, Claudius II Gothicus, Aurelian and Probus.

Evacuated c.271

First crossed the Danube under Severus Alexander (222-35

Dnieper

Dniester

EAST GOTHS

HERULI

King lends fleet to raiders 254

Cimmerian Bosphorus

Panticapaeum

Decius fell to Goths 251

L S

incum

DACIA

WEST GOTHS

ube

Abrittus

Black Sea

264

269

Marcianopolis

Trapezus

SASSANIAN

EMPIRE

Naïssus

Philippopolis

Byzantium

Chalcedon

BITHYNIA

Thessalonica

Pessinus

Ephesus

Sparta

Overrun by Goths 256

Victory of Gallienus over Goths 268

Captured by Goths from Decius (249-51)

Sacked by Goths in 253

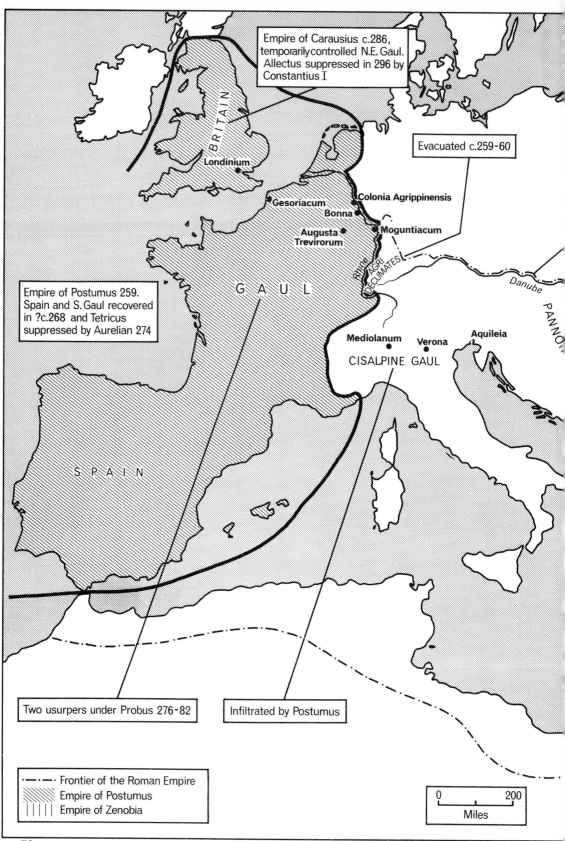

Empire of Carausius c.286, temporarily controlled N.E. Gaul. Allectus suppressed in 296 by Constantius I

Evacuated c.259-60

Empire of Postumus 259. Spain and S. Gaul recovered in ?c.268 and Tetricus suppressed by Aurelian 274

BRITAIN

Londinium

Gesoriacum

Colonia Agrippinensis

Bonna

Augusta Trevirorum

Moguntiacum

Rhine

AGRI DECUMATES

Danube

PANNO

G A U L

Mediolanum

Verona

Aquileia

CISALPINE GAUL

S P A I N

Two usurpers under Probus 276-82

Infiltrated by Postumus

—·—·—	Frontier of the Roman Empire
▨	Empire of Postumus
‖‖‖	Empire of Zenobia

0   200

Miles

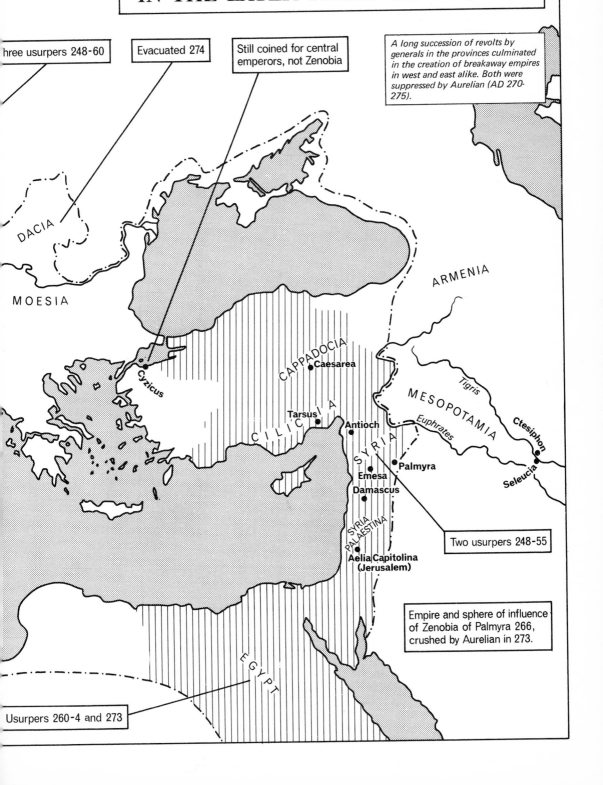

THE BREAKDOWN AND RECOVERY OF THE ROMAN EMPIRE IN THE LATER THIRD CENTURY A.D.

hree usurpers 248-60

Evacuated 274

Still coined for central emperors, not Zenobia

A long succession of revolts by generals in the provinces culminated in the creation of breakaway empires in west and east alike. Both were suppressed by Aurelian (AD 270-275).

DACIA

MOESIA

ARMENIA

CAPPADOCIA
Caesarea

Tigris

MESOPOTAMIA

Euphrates

Ctesiphon

Cyzicus

C I L I C I A

Tarsus

Antioch

S Y R I A

Palmyra

Seleucia

Emesa

Damascus

SYRIA
PALAESTINA

Two usurpers 248-55

Aelia Capitolina
(Jerusalem)

Empire and sphere of influence of Zenobia of Palmyra 266, crushed by Aurelian in 273.

E G Y P T

Usurpers 260-4 and 273

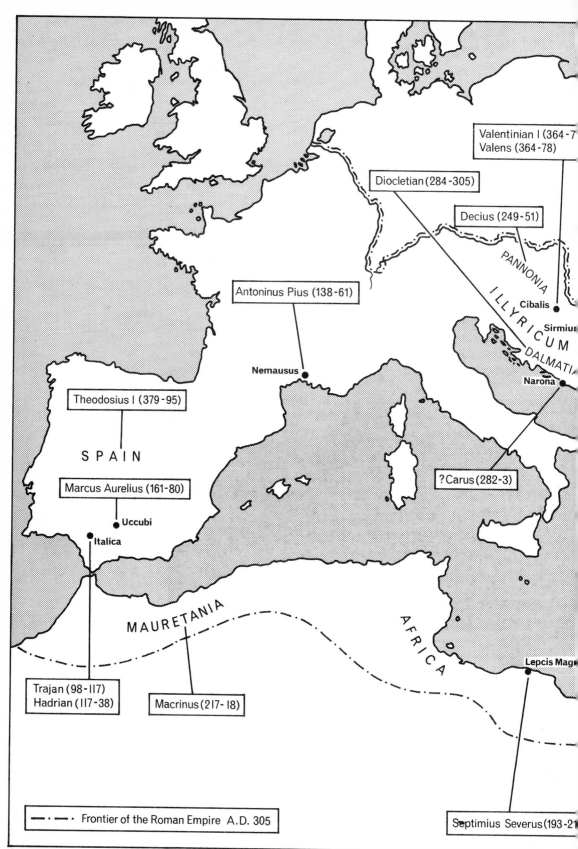

Valentinian I (364-7
Valens (364-78)

Diocletian (284-305)

Decius (249-51)

PANNONIA

ILLYRICUM

Cibalis

Sirmiu

Antoninus Pius (138-61)

DALMATIA

Narona

Theodosius I (379-95)

Nemausus

S P A I N

Marcus Aurelius (161-80)

?Carus (282-3)

Uccubi

Italica

MAURETANIA

AFRICA

Lepcis Mag

Trajan (98-117)
Hadrian (117-38)

Macrinus (217-18)

—·—·— Frontier of the Roman Empire A.D. 305

Septimius Severus (193-21

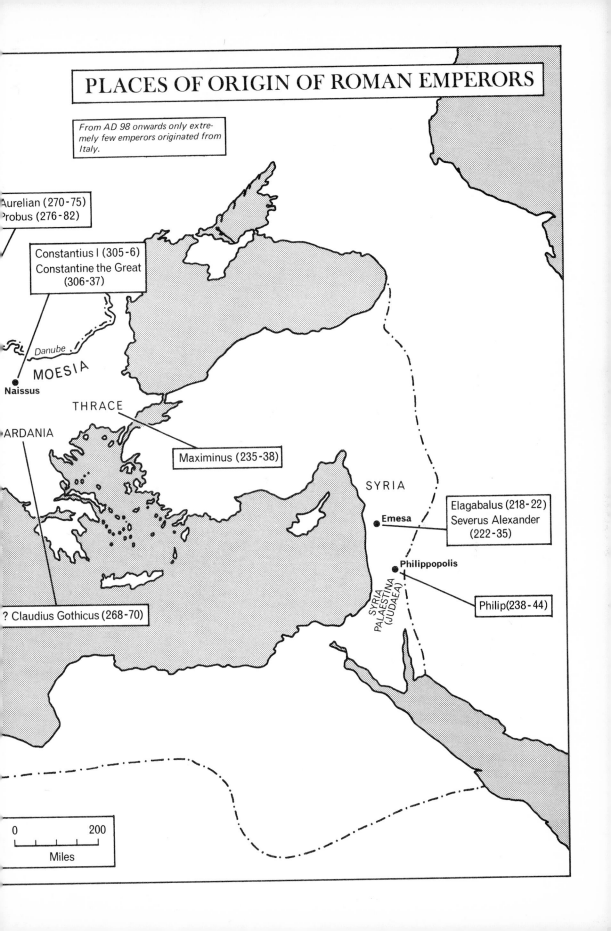

PLACES OF ORIGIN OF ROMAN EMPERORS

From AD 98 onwards only extremely few emperors originated from Italy.

Aurelian (270-75)
Probus (276-82)

Constantius I (305-6)
Constantine the Great
(306-37)

Danube

MOESIA

Naissus

THRACE

ARDANIA

Maximinus (235-38)

SYRIA

Emesa

Elagabalus (218-22)
Severus Alexander
(222-35)

Philippopolis

SYRIA
PALAESTINA
(JUDAEA)

Philip(238-44)

? Claudius Gothicus (268-70)

0   200

Miles

Areas of widespread Jewish settlement

● Towns with large Jewish communities

Jews deported from
Rome by Tiberius
A.D. 14 - 37

GERMANIA

Colonia

Rhine

Regina

Aquincum

PANNONIA

Mursa

Lutetia

Genabum

Vesontio

Alps

Tergeste

Ravenna

DALMATIA

Genua

ITALY

APULIA

GAUL

Burdigala

Tolosa

Pyrenees

Massilia

Rome

CALA

CAMPANIA

SPAIN

SARDINIA

Caralis

Panormus

SICILY

Corduba

Carthage

Melita

Gades

Volubilis

Oea

Atlas   Mountains

S A H A R A

0   250

Miles

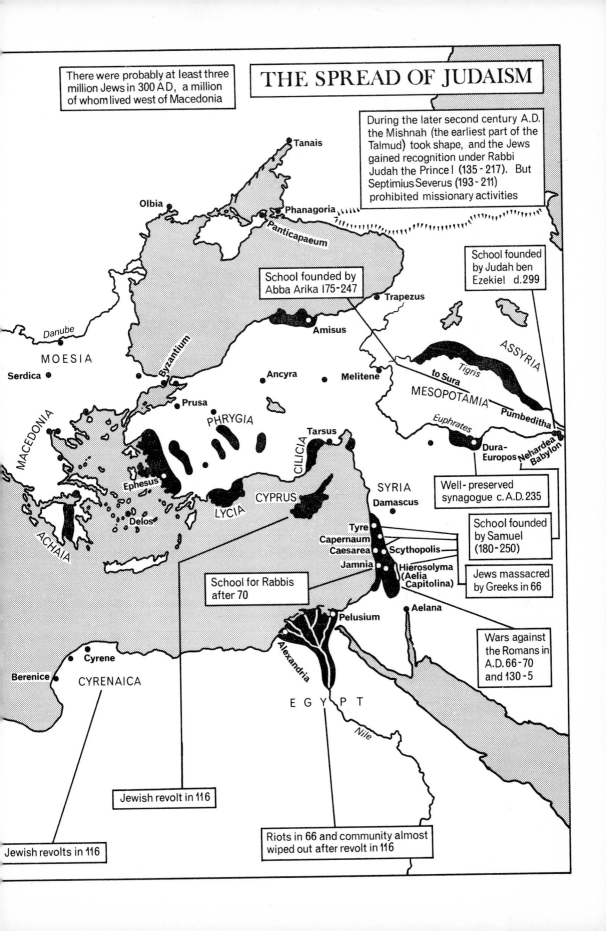

THE SPREAD OF JUDAISM

There were probably at least three million Jews in 300 A.D., a million of whom lived west of Macedonia

During the later second century A.D. the Mishnah (the earliest part of the Talmud) took shape, and the Jews gained recognition under Rabbi Judah the Prince I (135-217). But Septimius Severus (193-211) prohibited missionary activities

School founded by Judah ben Ezekiel d.299

School founded by Abba Arika 175-247

Well-preserved synagogue c.A.D. 235

School founded by Samuel (180-250)

Jews massacred by Greeks in 66

School for Rabbis after 70

Wars against the Romans in A.D. 66-70 and 130-5

Jewish revolt in 116

Jewish revolts in 116

Riots in 66 and community almost wiped out after revolt in 116

Tanais

Olbia

Phanagoria

Panticapaeum

Trapezus

Amisus

Danube

MOESIA

Serdica

Byzantium

Ancyra

Melitene

to Sura

MESOPOTAMIA

Tigris

ASSYRIA

Pumbeditha

Prusa

PHRYGIA

Tarsus

CILICIA

Euphrates

Dura-Europos

Nehardea

Babylon

Ephesus

CYPRUS

LYCIA

SYRIA

Damascus

Delos

MACEDONIA

ACHAIA

Tyre

Capernaum

Caesarea

Jamnia

Scythopolis

Hierosolyma (Aelia Capitolina)

Aelana

Pelusium

Cyrene

Berenice

CYRENAICA

Alexandria

E G Y P T

Nile

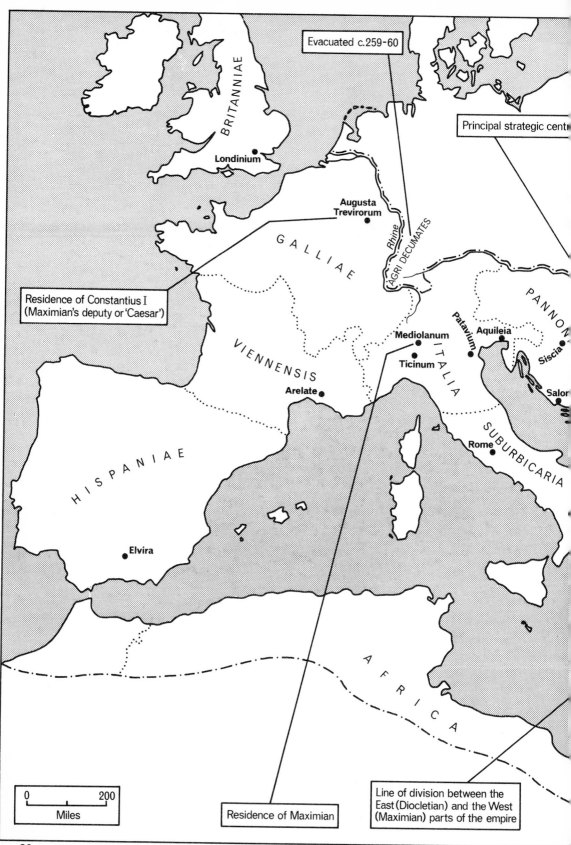

Evacuated c.259-60

Principal strategic centr[

Residence of Constantius I
(Maximian's deputy or 'Caesar')

BRITANNIAE

Londinium

Augusta
Trevirorum

GALLIAE

Rhine

AGRI DECUMATES

PANNON

VIENNENSIS

Mediolanum

Patavium

Aquileia

Siscia

Ticinum

ITALIA

Salor

Arelate

SUBURBICARIA

Rome

HISPANIAE

Elvira

AFRICA

0   200
Miles

Residence of Maximian

Line of division between the
East (Diocletian) and the West
(Maximian) parts of the empire

82

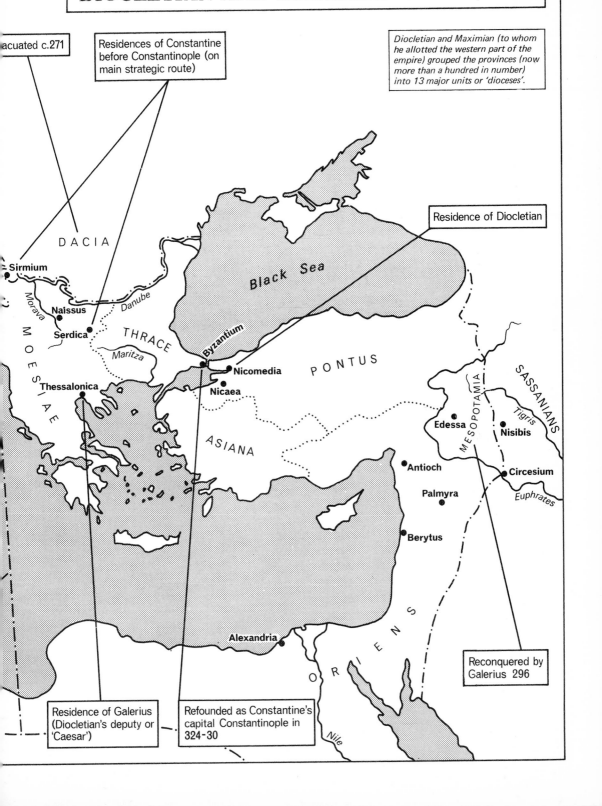

THE ROMAN EMPIRE UNDER DIOCLETIAN AND MAXIMIAN A.D. 284/6-305

acuated c.271

Residences of Constantine before Constantinople (on main strategic route)

Diocletian and Maximian (to whom he allotted the western part of the empire) grouped the provinces (now more than a hundred in number) into 13 major units or 'dioceses'.

Residence of Diocletian

Reconquered by Galerius 296

Residence of Galerius (Diocletian's deputy or 'Caesar')

Refounded as Constantine's capital Constantinople in 324-30

DACIA

Black Sea

Sirmium

Morava

Naissus

Danube

Serdica

THRACE

Maritza

Byzantium

PONTUS

Nicomedia

Nicaea

SASSANIANS

M O E S I A E

Thessalonica

ASIANA

Edessa

MESOPOTAMIA

Tigris

Nisibis

Circesium

Antioch

Palmyra

Euphrates

Berytus

O R I E N S

Alexandria

Nile

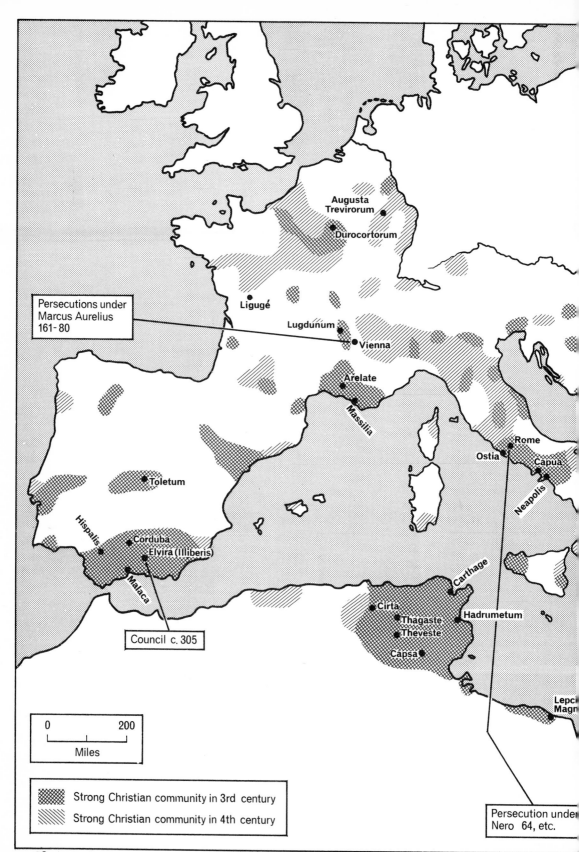

Persecutions under
Marcus Aurelius
161-80

Ligugé

Augusta
Trevirorum

Durocortorum

Lugdunum

Vienna

Arelate

Massilia

Rome

Ostia

Capua

Neapolis

Toletum

Hispalis

Corduba

Elvira (Illiberis)

Malaca

Council c. 305

Carthage

Cirta

Thagaste

Theveste

Hadrumetum

Capsa

Lepcis
Magna

0   200
Miles

Strong Christian community in 3rd century

Strong Christian community in 4th century

Persecution under
Nero 64, etc.

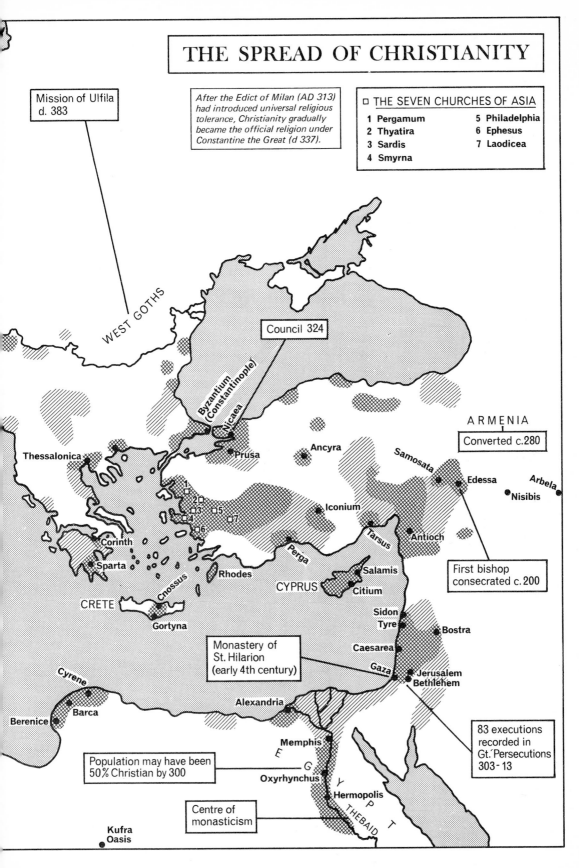

THE SPREAD OF CHRISTIANITY

Mission of Ulfila
d. 383

After the Edict of Milan (AD 313) had introduced universal religious tolerance, Christianity gradually became the official religion under Constantine the Great (d 337).

□ THE SEVEN CHURCHES OF ASIA

1 Pergamum   5 Philadelphia
2 Thyatira   6 Ephesus
3 Sardis   7 Laodicea
4 Smyrna

WEST GOTHS

Council 324

Byzantium
(Constantinople)
Nicaea

ARMENIA
Converted c.280

Thessalonica

Prusa

Ancyra

Samosata

Edessa

Arbela

Nisibis

1
2
3 5
4 6 7

Iconium

Tarsus

Antioch

First bishop
consecrated c.200

Corinth

Sparta

Cnossus

Rhodes

Perga

CYPRUS

Salamis

Citium

CRETE

Gortyna

Sidon
Tyre

Bostra

Caesarea

Monastery of
St. Hilarion
(early 4th century)

Gaza

Jerusalem
Bethlehem

Cyrene

Barca

Berenice

Alexandria

83 executions
recorded in
Gt. Persecutions
303 - 13

Memphis

E
G
Y
P
T

Population may have been
50% Christian by 300

Oxyrhynchus

Hermopolis

THEBAID

Centre of
monasticism

Kufra
Oasis

H

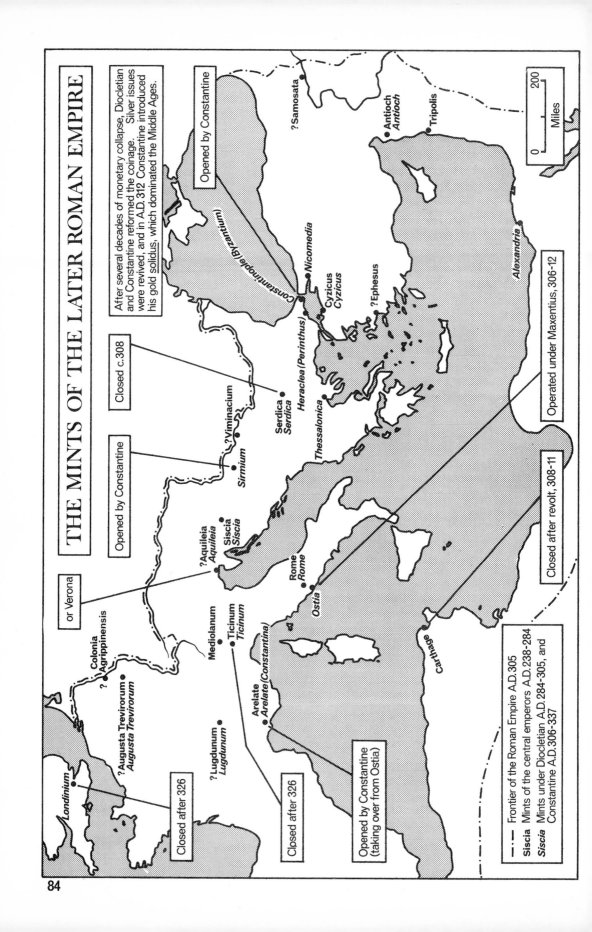

THE MINTS OF THE LATER ROMAN EMPIRE

After several decades of monetary collapse, Diocletian and Constantine reformed the coinage. Silver issues were revived, and in A.D.312 Constantine introduced his gold solidus, which dominated the Middle Ages.

Opened by Constantine

Closed c.308

Opened by Constantine

or Verona

Closed after 326

Closed after 326

Opened by Constantine (taking over from Ostia)

Operated under Maxentius, 306-12

Closed after revolt, 308-11

Colonia Agrippinensis

?Augusta Treverorum
Augusta Treverorum

?Lugdunum
Lugdunum

Londinium

Mediolanum

Ticinum
Ticinum

Arelate
Arelate (Constantina)

?Aquileia
Aquileia

Siscia
Siscia

Rome
Rome

Ostia

Carthage

?Viminacium

Sirmium

Serdica
Serdica

Thessalonica

Heraclea (Perinthus)

Constantinople (Byzantium)

Nicomedia

Cyzicus
Cyzicus

?Ephesus

?Samosata

Antioch
Antioch

Tripolis

Alexandria

--- Frontier of the Roman Empire A.D.305

Siscia Mints of the central emperors A.D.238-284

Siscia Mints under Diocletian A.D. 284-305, and Constantine A.D.306-337

0   200
Miles

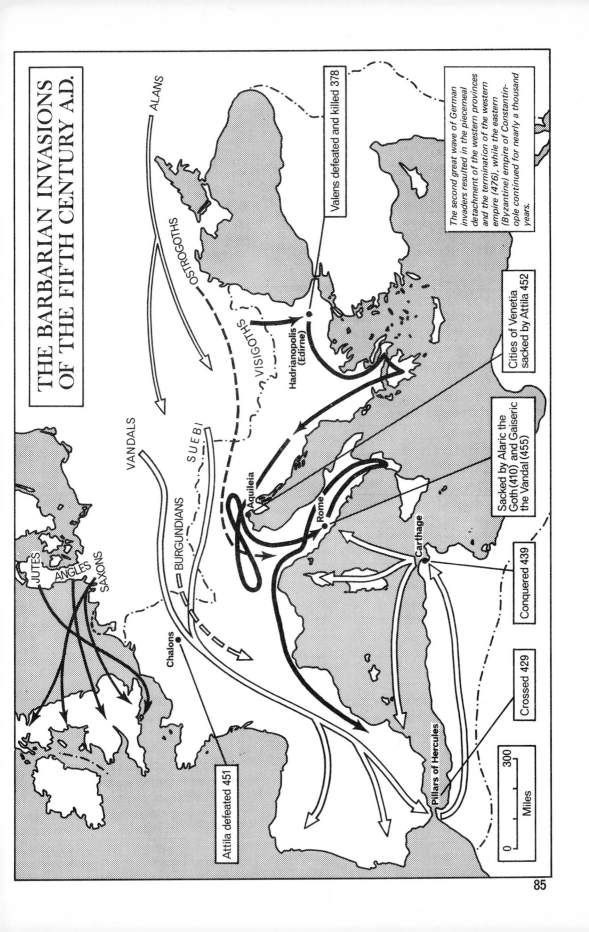

THE BARBARIAN INVASIONS OF THE FIFTH CENTURY A.D.

ALANS

OSTROGOTHS

Valens defeated and killed 378

The second great wave of German invaders resulted in the piecemeal detachment of the western provinces and the termination of the western empire (476), while the eastern (Byzantine) empire of Constantinople continued for nearly a thousand years.

VISIGOTHS

Hadrianopolis (Edirne)

VANDALS

SUEBI

Aquileia

Rome

Cities of Venetia sacked by Attila 452

BURGUNDIANS

JUTES

ANGLES

SAXONS

Chalons

Carthage

Sacked by Alaric the Goth (410) and Gaiseric the Vandal (455)

Conquered 439

Crossed 429

Attila defeated 451

Pillars of Hercules

300

0

Miles

85

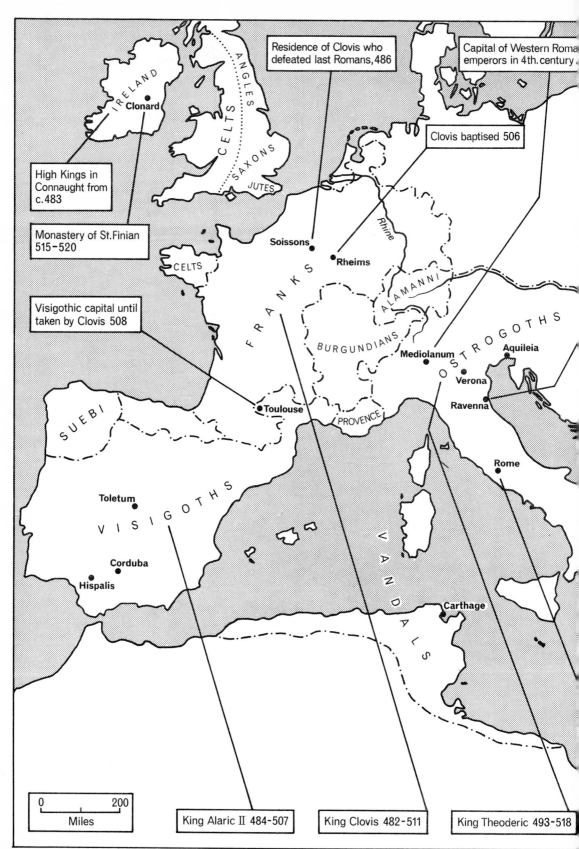

Residence of Clovis who defeated last Romans, 486

Capital of Western Roman emperors in 4th century

Clovis baptised 506

High Kings in Connaught from c.483

Monastery of St.Finian 515-520

Visigothic capital until taken by Clovis 508

IRELAND

Clonard

CELTS

ANGLES

SAXONS

JUTES

CELTS

F R A N K S

Soissons

Rheims

Rhine

A L A M A N N I

BURGUNDIANS

Toulouse

PROVENCE

O S T R O G O T H S

Mediolanum

Verona

Aquileia

Ravenna

Rome

S U E B I

Toletum

V I S I G O T H S

Corduba

Hispalis

V A N D A L S

Carthage

0   200

Miles

King Alaric II 484-507

King Clovis 482-511

King Theoderic 493-518

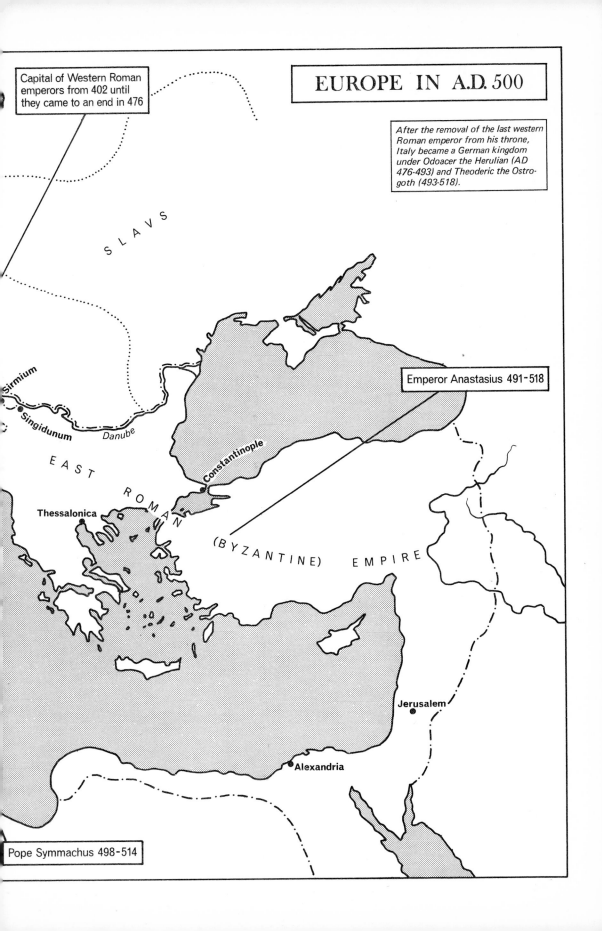

EUROPE IN A.D. 500

Capital of Western Roman emperors from 402 until they came to an end in 476

After the removal of the last western Roman emperor from his throne, Italy became a German kingdom under Odoacer the Herulian (AD 476-493) and Theoderic the Ostrogoth (493-518).

SLAVS

Sirmium

Singidunum

Danube

EAST

ROMAN

Thessalonica

Constantinople

(BYZANTINE) EMPIRE

Emperor Anastasius 491-518

Jerusalem

Alexandria

Pope Symmachus 498-514

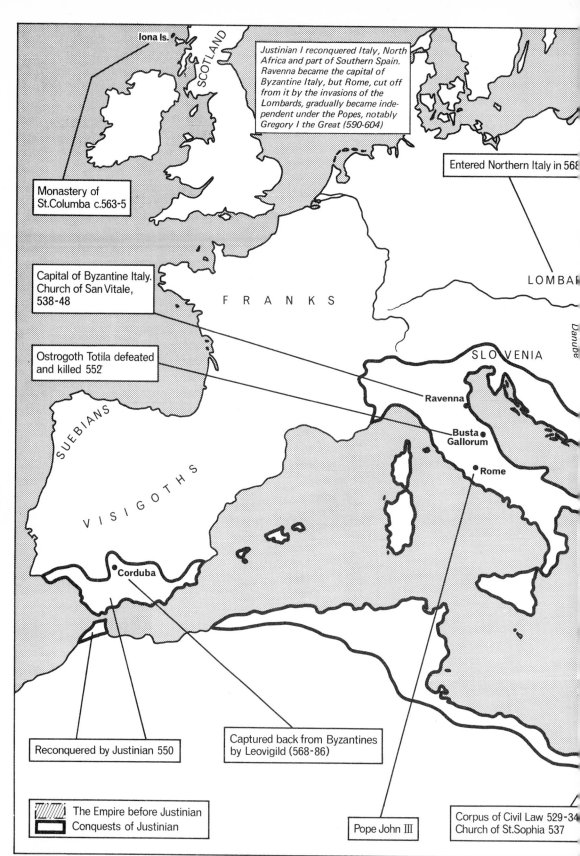

Iona Is.

SCOTLAND

Justinian I reconquered Italy, North
Africa and part of Southern Spain.
Ravenna became the capital of
Byzantine Italy, but Rome, cut off
from it by the invasions of the
Lombards, gradually became inde-
pendent under the Popes, notably
Gregory I the Great (590-604)

Entered Northern Italy in 568

Monastery of
St.Columba c.563-5

LOMBA

Capital of Byzantine Italy.
Church of San Vitale,
538-48

F R A N K S

Danube

SLOVENIA

Ostrogoth Totila defeated
and killed 552

Ravenna

Busta
Gallorum

SUEBIANS

Rome

V I S I G O T H S

Corduba

Reconquered by Justinian 550

Captured back from Byzantines
by Leovigild (568-86)

The Empire before Justinian
Conquests of Justinian

Pope John III

Corpus of Civil Law 529-34
Church of St.Sophia 537

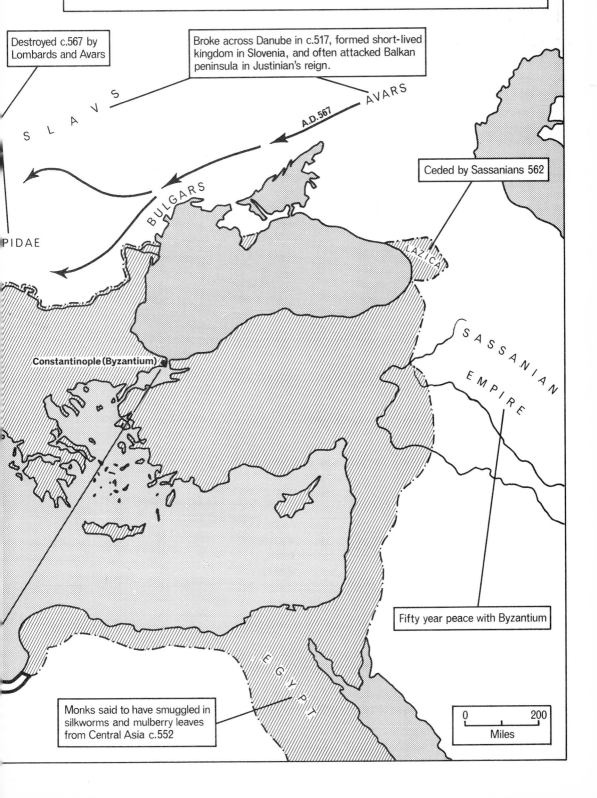

THE BYZANTINE EMPIRE OF JUSTINIAN I
(A.D. 527-65)

Destroyed c.567 by Lombards and Avars

Broke across Danube in c.517, formed short-lived kingdom in Slovenia, and often attacked Balkan peninsula in Justinian's reign.

Ceded by Sassanians 562

S L A V S

A.D. 567

AVARS

BULGARS

PIDAE

LAZICA

Constantinople (Byzantium)

S A S S A N I A N

E M P I R E

Fifty year peace with Byzantium

E G Y P T

Monks said to have smuggled in silkworms and mulberry leaves from Central Asia c.552

0   200
Miles

Index of Place Names[1]

Modern names are given in brackets

[1] I have sometimes sacrificed consistency of spelling to convenience and tradition.